JEFFERSON AND
EDUCATION

JEFFERSON AND
EDUCATION

by Jennings L. Wagoner, Jr.

Preface by William G. Bowen

THOMAS JEFFERSON FOUNDATION

Monticello Monograph Series

2004

Library of Congress Cataloging-in-Publication Data

Wagoner, Jennings L.
  Jefferson and education / by Jennings L. Wagoner, Jr. ; preface by William G. Bowen.
     p. cm. -- (Monticello monographs series)
Includes bibliographical references and index.
  ISBN 1-882886-24-0
  1. Jefferson, Thomas, 1743-1826--Political and social views. 2. Jefferson, Thomas, 1743-1826-
-Knowledge and learning. 3. Jefferson, Thomas, 1743-1826--Influence. 4. Education--United
States--History--18th century. 5. Education--Virginia--History--18th century. 6. University of
Virginia--History. I. Title. II. Series.
E332.2.W34 2004
973.4'6'092--dc22

                                                                           2004017013

ON THE COVER

Inset image: Rotunda at the University of Virginia. (Courtesy Bill Sublette, University of Virginia).
Background image: Thomas Jefferson's letter to Peter Carr, September 7, 1814. (Courtesy Library of
Congress).

Copyright © 2004 by Thomas Jefferson Foundation, Inc.

Designed by Gibson Design Associates.
Edited and coordinated by Beth L. Cheuk.

This book was made possible by support from the
Martin S. and Luella Davis Publications Endowment.

Distributed by
The University of North Carolina Press
Chapel Hill, North Carolina 27515-2288
1-800-848-6224

For Morgan, Caroline, Katherine, and Will

Thomas Jefferson Foundation, Inc.

CONTENTS

Thomas Jefferson *by Thomas Sully (1821). (Courtesy West Point Museum Art Collection, United States Military Academy)*

PREFACE

Near the end of this wonderful book, Jennings Wagoner writes: "While Jefferson was in some ways a product of his time, he was most significantly *the prophet of later times*." This astute observation is the principal theme of my preface. This book will resonate with anyone who has spent time in a major research university—and especially anyone who has had responsibility for participating in the leadership of one of these rather odd institutions (as faculty member, administrator, or trustee/regent). The book reminds us of how far-sighted Jefferson was in the issues he chose to address, in the goals that he set, and in the solutions that he proposed. It is as if he were among us today, debating many of the same questions. And how much we would benefit right now from his wisdom, his academic insight and political sophistication, and his determination.

At the center of Jefferson's thinking about education were two propositions that most of us would embrace today:

- First, that "educational theory was inseparable from political theory," and that the survival of a democratic/republican form of government depended on an educated populace that would be "virtuous and vigilant."
- Second, that freedom in all of its forms—political freedom, religious freedom, and intellectual freedom—was essential to both a sound educational system and a well-functioning "republican polity."

One of the hallmarks of our system of higher education is its commitment to what we call today "academic freedom," and there is no more eloquent statement of what this means than Jefferson's insistence that "This institution [the University of Virginia] will be based on the illimitable freedom of the human mind. For here we are not afraid to follow truth wherever it may lead, nor [afraid to] tolerate any error so long as reason is left free to combat it."[1] We are prone to take our freedoms for granted, and it is easy to forget that the long history of higher education around the world is replete with instances of efforts to impose thought control by states or religions.[2]

Jefferson also anticipated a major contemporary concern when he emphasized that a solid precollegiate system of education was essential for the nation and the advancement of an educated citizenry. His advocacy of public support of education below the university level (though more limited in conception than what we would expect today) was well ahead of his time, even though he failed in his efforts to pass his Bill for the More General Diffusion of Knowledge. Today prospects for the continuing excellence of American higher education depend in no small degree on our ability to improve precollegiate education, and especially the "preparedness" of students from disadvantaged backgrounds.

In thinking about education at the university level, and in considering innumerable curricular proposals, Jefferson was also "modern" in the heavy emphasis he placed on cultivation of the "useful sciences" and on teaching subjects at their highest level. Department chairs, provosts, and presidents will identify with the descriptions Professor Wagoner provides of Jefferson's determined efforts to recruit absolutely outstanding faculty—including faculty from abroad—to set the right standard. The failures of many of these searches are also useful reminders that it was never easy to attract just the right academic leadership.

Nor was it ever inexpensive. Jefferson understood well the need to spend money to achieve excellence (including architectural distinction, as reflected in his "academical village"), and the accounts of his fundraising efforts and the attendant frustrations will resonate with the leaders of private and public universities today. (Jefferson complained that his efforts were being countered by "ignorance, malice, egotism," political and religious "fanaticism," and "local perversities." A list with which many of us can identify!)

"Mr. Jefferson's University" did not just spring into being overnight. One further lesson to be gleaned from this history is how important it has always been to have powerful allies—Madison and Monroe both served with Jefferson on the board of Central College, the predecessor to the University of Virginia—and loyal friends, such as Joseph Cabell (the real hero of this story, along with Jefferson), willing to work endless hours to persuade legislators to do the right thing. The related lesson is that there is no substitute for persistence. The account provided here of the long struggle to establish the University of Virginia has all the trappings of a thriller, with end point unknown, that has more than its share of ups and downs. Jefferson's determination to "stay the course," to not give up his first principles, is well worth remembering, especially when one's opponents are powerful and the odds against success seem high.

Jefferson's forward thinking did not, as everyone knows, extend to embracing the kind of racial inclusiveness that is so important in American life in the twenty-first century. As Professor Wagoner puts it, Jefferson was "limited by his own and his society's assumptions." Jefferson's attitudes toward African Americans (and especially his conviction that they could never live alongside whites in America) seem today—unlike his views on almost all other subjects—locked in a time capsule. But Jefferson is hardly alone among founders of great universities in this regard. I think immediately of South Africa, and of the University of Cape Town, which was founded by Cecil Rhodes. At her installation as Vice Chancellor of UCT in 1996, Mamphela Ramphele (a South African woman born in the Northern Transvaal and a leader of the anti-apartheid resistance movement), set out to "lay to rest the ghosts of the past." She paid tribute to the vision and foresight individuals such as Cecil Rhodes contributed to the founding of "this illustrious institution;" and then she added: "It is sad that their vision failed to acknowledge the inhumanity of racism and sexism." Still, she concluded, "let them rest;" "they must find peace alongside the ghosts ... of other people whose intellectual contributions to South Africa were curtailed by racism and sexism."[3]

I end by returning to the forward-looking theme of freedom of thought with which I began. Professor Wagoner wisely suggests that "Perhaps Jefferson's most enduring legacy is the dictum that the current generation must chart its own course in matters educational as in other ways." Jefferson is quoted as saying that: "Laws and institutions must go hand in hand with the progress of the human mind.... Institutions must keep pace with the times.... [No] civilized society [should] remain ever under the regimen of their barbarous ancestors." On my desk is an alabaster calendar inscribed with a saying by Burroughs that is one of my favorites: "New times always! Old time we cannot keep." Jefferson said the same thing nearly two centuries ago.

— WILLIAM G. BOWEN, PRESIDENT
The Andrew W. Mellon Foundation

---

[1] Professor Wagoner is at his scholarly best when he goes on to add the qualification that not even Jefferson was above considering the political persuasions of candidates for the professor of law at the university (pp. 135-138).

[2] See, for example, Bernard Lewis's masterful *The Jews of Islam*, in which he observes: "Tolerance is a new virtue, intolerance a new crime…. Until comparatively modern times, Christian Europe neither prized nor practiced tolerance itself, and was not greatly offended by its absence in others. The charge that was always brought against Islam was not that its doctrines were imposed by force—something seen as normal and natural—but that its doctrines were false." Experiences in modern times in countries as different as China, Chile, and Greece are sober reminders of how easy it is for universities to lose essential freedoms.

[3] "Embracing the Future," installation address by Mamphela Ramphele, 11/10/1996.

PROLOGUE

*T*homas Jefferson was clear about the way in which he wished to be remembered by posterity. In sketching the design for his tombstone in his last days, Jefferson noted that he wanted only three items as his epitaph: "Author of the Declaration of American Independence, Of the Statute of Virginia for Religious Freedom, and Father of the University of Virginia." Political freedom, religious freedom, and intellectual freedom; these were the touchstones of Jefferson's life and work. These he hoped would be remembered as his most important and enduring contributions to his countrymen.

The University of Virginia, termed by Jefferson as the "last service I can render my country" and the "last of my mortal cares," was indeed a remarkable achievement. It stands today as a lasting tribute to Jefferson's faith in the power of education and his belief that education was of central importance in insuring the very survival of the new nation whose birth he had so boldly proclaimed in July of 1776. However, the beauty and power of "Mr. Jefferson's University," perhaps surpassed only by the eloquence of his Declaration, are often allowed to overshadow Jefferson's equally earnest commitment to the general education of the mass of the population. While struggling to obtain funds to complete the University of Virginia, Jefferson also professed that, if forced to choose between establishing a system of general education and finishing the university, "I would rather abandon the last, because it is safer to have a whole people respectably enlightened, than a few in a high state of science [knowledge], and the many in ignorance." European nations, he added, had provided ample demonstration that the latter alternative "is the most dangerous state in which a nation can be." In a similar vein he had noted a few years earlier: "A system of general instruction, which shall reach every description of our citizens, from the richest to the poorest, as it was the earliest, so will it be the latest, of all the public concerns which I shall permit myself to take an interest."[1]

As will be discussed in the pages that follow, Jefferson's efforts to advance educational opportunities for both the rank and file and the most promising of the citizenry were at times compromised by pragmatic political strategies deemed necessary to advance other, equally pressing, ideals. But there is no gainsaying his fundamental conviction that, "If a nation expects to be ignorant and free, in a state of civilization, it expects what never was and never will be." Moreover, Jefferson consistently maintained that in a republican-democratic society, the education of the common people must be provided for. As he put the matter in 1789: "Wherever the people are well-informed, they can be trusted with their own government. Whenever things get so far wrong as to attract their notice, they may be relied on to set them to rights."[2]

But why did Thomas Jefferson, born into the ranks of the Virginia gentry, embrace such views? What motivated him to work for over forty years to urge his native state to adopt a plan that would provide for publicly supported education for all citizens as well as a powerful state university that would offer education at the highest level to the best and brightest of each generation? And why was Jefferson, esteemed architect of the founding principles on which this nation was built, unable in the end to see his vision completed in full? How was it that Jefferson was able to secure the founding of the University of Virginia as the *capstone* of a hierarchical educational system but yet unable to gain sufficient support for putting in place publicly supported elementary and secondary schools as the *cornerstones* of the system? To search out the answers to these questions is to understand the contours of Jefferson's labors on behalf of, and his commitment to, education in the new American nation.

Jefferson's self-designed tombstone at Monticello. (Thomas Jefferson Foundation)

Thomas Jefferson *by Moses Ezekiel (1910) in front of the North Portico of the Rotunda at the University of Virginia. (Courtesy Bill Sublette, University of Virginia)*

Chapter One

THE EDUCATION OF A PLANTER

It is highly interesting to our country, and it is the duty of its functionaries,
to provide that every citizen in it should receive an education proportioned
to the condition and pursuits of his life.

— THOMAS JEFFERSON TO PETER CARR, 1814[3]

On the face of it, there would seem to be little reason for Thomas Jefferson to have concerned himself with education. After all, his own education was conventional enough for the day—conventional, that is, if one had the good fortune of being born into a family with the financial means and motivation to provide for private teachers and boarding schools. The educational arrangements for children in colonial Virginia reflected long-standing European tradition, and the prevailing attitude was perhaps most clearly expressed by the colony's Royal Governor, Sir William Berkeley, in 1671. Reporting to the Commissioners of Trade and Plantations back in England on conditions in the colony, Berkeley explained that with respect to education, Virginians were following "the same course that is taken in England out of towns; every man according to his own ability in instructing his children."[4]

"Every man according to his own ability" meant, of course, that the economically secure could provide much better for their children than could colonists of more humble circumstances. Children of poorer families learned whatever they could from their parents or perhaps engaged in an apprenticeship to gain skills in some craft or trade thought suitable to their station in life. Here and there some children gained a semblance of literacy from a neighboring minister or under the guidance of a teacher in an "old field school" or "pay school," typically a log or frame building erected in an exhausted and abandoned tobacco field. Itinerant teachers for these schools were irregularly supported by a few neighboring families whose proximity and interest enabled them to provide for at least a smattering of formal education for their children. In more populated areas, instruction was sometimes made possible by the generosity of a benevolent soul who made provision in a will for a "free school" for the poor children who lived in the vicinity. But schools such as these were typically considered to be "pauper" or "charity" schools, and parents with pride or any pretensions to favored standing in society looked upon such "public" institutions with scorn. Indeed, Governor Berkeley exaggerated only a little when he proclaimed that, "Thank God, there are no free schools nor printing [in Virginia]" and added that: "I hope we shall not have these [for a] hundred years; for learning has brought disobedience and heresy, and sects into the world, and printing has divulged them, and libels against the best government. God keep us from both."[5]

It was just over a hundred years later that Thomas Jefferson, then a young legislator on the verge of becoming governor of Virginia himself, introduced into the Virginia legislature a bill that, if successful, would in fact have established publicly funded "free" schools throughout the Commonwealth of Virginia. Governor Berkeley had disappeared from the scene, but attitudes such as he professed were still very much in currency. Beginning in the 1770s and continuing until his death in 1826, Thomas Jefferson encouraged the very kinds of political, religious, and educational "disobedience and heresy" so feared by Berkeley. As Jefferson grew to question the political and religious orthodoxies of the day, so too did he openly challenge the prevailing social and educational assumptions upon which colonial society had been based.

Piedmont Virginia was sparsely settled when Jefferson was born on April 13, 1743, and his home at Shadwell, in the district that became Albemarle County, was a rather modest frame dwelling. From the higher ridges of the low mountains surrounding Shadwell one could see the lofty Blue Ridge range rising in the west. Although Shadwell was on the edge of what was then Virginia's western frontier and Jefferson's father, Peter, was a surveyor who had been one of the first pioneers to settle in the region, the circumstances of Jefferson's childhood were far from impoverished. As the third child and first son of Peter and Jane Randolph Jefferson, Thomas fell heir not only to favored social standing and in due course a share of impressive family property holdings, but also was afforded the educational advantages reserved for the Virginia gentry.

According to family tradition, one of Thomas Jefferson's earliest childhood recollections was that of being carried on a pillow by a slave mounted on horseback as the Jefferson family made its way eastward from Shadwell to Tuckahoe, a plantation on the James River. Because the master of Tuckahoe, William Randolph, a long-time friend of Peter Jefferson (and his wife's cousin), had recently died, Peter Jefferson moved his family to this more established plantation. There he assumed the supervision of the estate and care of the Randolph children as had been requested by Colonel Randolph before his death. By the time Thomas had reached his fifth birthday, his father had hired a tutor to undertake the instruction of William Randolph's son, Thomas Mann Randolph, his two sisters, and the Jefferson children. Thus, in a small frame building on the Tuckahoe estate, Thomas Jefferson, along with his sisters and Randolph cousins, began his formal

Jefferson's Schoolhouse at Tuckahoe Plantation *(1993) by M. W. Stafford. (Courtesy of author)*

educational journey with instruction in the fundamentals of reading, writing, and arithmetic. Perhaps Jefferson's lessons in music and dancing began while at Tuckahoe; they clearly had become an important part of his education during his boarding school years when his favorite indoor amusement was playing the violin. Home life as well as schooling provided instruction in the morals, manners, and social graces attendant to genteel plantation life, while the countryside exposed young Jefferson and his kin to the wonders of nature and the challenges of outdoor life. By privilege of birth and early education, Thomas Jefferson was being properly groomed to take his place among the Virginia gentry.[6]

Thomas Jefferson was nine years old in 1752 when his family moved back to Shadwell and a new phase of his education began. In that year Peter Jefferson placed his son in the Latin school of the Reverend William Douglas, a recently arrived émigré from Scotland. As was the custom, Jefferson boarded at the clergy-man's home with a few other boys when school was in session. In later life Jefferson described Douglas as being a "superficial Latinist" and indicated that he knew even less about Greek, but nonetheless credited the minister with instructing him in the rudiments of those languages along with a beginning knowledge of French—albeit probably laced with a Scottish accent.[7]

Thomas Jefferson was just a few months beyond his fourteenth birthday when his father died at the untimely age of forty-nine. The desk, books, bookcases, maps, surveying instruments, and other items bequeathed to his first-born son perished in a fire that destroyed Shadwell some years later, but one provision in Peter's will made it possible for young Thomas to gain possession of what became to him the most prized object his father could have provided: the means to acquire a complete classical education. In accordance with his father's instructions, in early 1758 Thomas enrolled in the more advanced grammar or secondary school of the Reverend James Maury, "a correct classical scholar." While boarding with the minister's family, Thomas learned to read Greek and Latin authors in the original, a practice of "sublime luxury" that he continued throughout his life. Maury also provided Jefferson with instruction in mathematics, history, and geography and encouraged an interest in modern and ancient literature.[8]

A few months before reaching the age of seventeen, Jefferson informed his guardians of his desire to further his education and widen his circle of acquaintances by enrolling at the College of William and Mary. In the early spring of 1760, young Jefferson left the hills of Piedmont Virginia and traveled eastward to the capital at Williamsburg. Although Williamsburg was the largest town Jefferson had then seen, the entire community covered only a square mile and, except when the Assembly was in session, numbered fewer than two thousand inhabitants. The main college building, designed by Christopher Wren, was impressive enough, but the institution itself was in turmoil when Jefferson began his studies. Death, dissipation, and disorder had temporarily reduced the usual complement of a president and six professors to two by the time of Jefferson's arrival. The newest member of the faculty was Dr. William Small, a graduate of Marischal College of the University of Edinburgh. Small, the only professor to enlist Jefferson's admiration and affection, was also the only member of the faculty who was not an Anglican minister.[9]

Portrait of William Small (artist and date unknown). (Courtesy Mr. David L. Craig of Brisbane, Australia)

William Small proved to be an important element in Jefferson's education. Small made Jefferson his daily companion and from him, Jefferson later noted, "I got my first views of the expansion of science, and of the system of things in which we are placed." In effect, Small *was* William and Mary for Jefferson, since except for a few months, Small was his only regular teacher. Small quickened Jefferson's interest in Enlightenment philosophy and the useful sciences, and, as the only layman on the faculty, no doubt contributed to his growing anticlericalism as well.[10]

Small figured importantly in Jefferson's intellectual development in yet another important way. It was through Small that Jefferson developed a lasting friendship with George Wythe, a prominent jurist under whom Jefferson studied law for five years after completing college. In devoting himself to the private

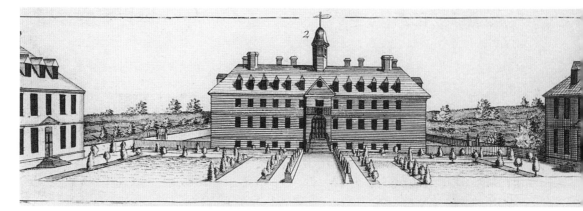

Detail from Bodleian Plate *showing the Sir Christopher Wren Building at the College of William and Mary. (Courtesy Colonial Williamsburg Foundation)*

study of law, Jefferson was following the approved procedure for those who did not venture to England for legal training. Not until the Revolutionary period did formal legal instruction begin in the United States, and it was Wythe himself who, through arrangements made by Jefferson as governor and member of the Board of Visitors of the College of William and Mary, assumed the first law professorship in the country in 1779 by giving lectures on the subject at Jefferson's alma mater.

Still another individual who contributed significantly to Jefferson's social and political development was the Royal Governor of Virginia, Francis Fauquier. Fauquier, later praised by Jefferson as "the ablest man who had ever filled [that office]," frequently invited Jefferson to the palace for dinner, conversation, and musical performances. "At these dinners," Jefferson remarked years afterward, "I have heard more good sense, more rational and philosophical conversations, than in all my life besides." The governor's reputation as a man of taste, refinement, and erudition clearly impressed Jefferson, and though he was critical of the vices that accompanied the social life of the Tidewater elite, just as he had shied away from the extravagant gambling, heavy drinking, and occasional riotous behavior of some of his college chums, he could later recall Williamsburg as "the finest school of manners and morals that ever existed in America."[11]

For Jefferson no doubt it was. As one who could "tear himself away from his dearest friends, to fly to his studies," and as one who hated indolence and became a penetrating critic of the society in which he was nurtured, Jefferson was perhaps uniquely suited to make the most of his Williamsburg experiences. Although clearly not a self-made man on the style of his compatriot, Benjamin Franklin, like the elder statesman, Jefferson also possessed the ability to turn varied experiences into lessons on the proper conduct of life. Some years later in giving advice to his daughter Martha, Jefferson penned a phrase that the creator of *Poor Richard* could fully appreciate: "No person will have occasion to complain of the want of time who never loses any." And as his own life's history was to demonstrate, Jefferson observed further: "It is wonderful how much may be done if we are always doing."[12]

By all accounts, Jefferson was "doing" steadily at Williamsburg. Through his association with Governor Fauquier, Jefferson met other public officials and leading politicians and frequently attended sessions of the General Court. It was while standing in the doorway of the Chamber of Burgesses on May 30, 1765, that the twenty-two-year-old Jefferson heard Patrick Henry denounce the Stamp Act in terms that brought cries of "Treason!" from the floor. The fiery orator's blast against the policies of the crown made a deep impression upon the young law student who in brief time would also enlist his energies in the same cause. Williamsburg was indeed a school of manners and morals. For Jefferson it became a school of enlightened political awareness as well.[13]

however, in our zeal for their maintenance, we may be perplexed & differ-
iate, as to the structures of society most likely to secure them.

In the constitution of Spain as proposed by the late Cortes,
there was a principle entirely new to me, and not noticed in yours, that
no person born after that day, should ever acquire the rights of citizenship until he could read and write. it is impossible sufficiently
to estimate the wisdom of this provision. of all those which have been
thought of for securing fidelity in the administration of the government, constant reliance to the principles of the constitution, and
progressive amendments with the progressive advances of the human
mind, or changes in human affairs, it is the most effectual. enlighten
the people generally, and tyranny and oppressions of body & mind
will vanish like evil spirits at the dawn of day. altho' I do not,
with some enthusiasts, believe that the human condition will ever
advance to such a state of perfection as that there shall no longer
be pain or vice in the world, yet I believe it susceptible of much
improvement, and, most of all, in matters of government and
religion; and that the diffusion of knowledge among the people
is to be the instrument by which it is to be effected. the consti-
-tution of the Cortes had defects enough; but when I saw in it this
amendatory provision, I was satisfied all would come right in
time, under it's salutary operation. no people have more need
of a similar provision than those for whom you have felt so
much interest. no mortal wishes them more success than I do.
but if what I have heard of the ignorance & bigotry of the mass
be true, I doubt their capacity to understand and to support
a free government; and fear that their emancipation from the
foreign tyranny of Spain will result in a military despotism at
home. Palacios may be great; others may be great; but it is
the multitude which possesses force; and wisdom must yield to that.

Page four from Thomas Jefferson's letter to P. S. Du Pont, April 24, 1816. (Courtesy Library of Congress)

Chapter Two

Enlightenment and the Progress of Mankind

Enlighten the people generally and tyranny and oppressions of body and mind will vanish like evil spirits at the dawn of day. Although I do not, with some enthusiasts, believe that the human condition will ever advance to such a state of perfection as that there shall no longer be pain or vice in the world, yet I believe it susceptible of much improvement, and most of all in matters of government and religion; and that the diffusion of knowledge among the people is to be the instrument by which it is to be effected.

— Thomas Jefferson to Pierre Samuel Du Pont de Nemours, 1816[14]

Thomas Jefferson had by no means completed his education when he began to practice law at the age of twenty-three. His studies and associations while in Williamsburg had but baptized Jefferson into the intellectual and political climate of the Enlightenment. He continued to seek knowledge wherever it might be found and at the age of seventy-six could still describe himself as "a hard student." In conversation, in correspondence, via observation and experimentation, and always through reading, he endeavored to enlarge his understanding of the universal laws he believed were awaiting discovery.[15]

An avid collector of books, Jefferson amassed three libraries during his lifetime. His first library, begun with forty books he had inherited from his father, was lost with the burning of his home at Shadwell in 1770. For the next forty-five years he carefully built up another, gathering books from Europe as well as America and cataloguing each according to the paradigm of universal knowledge developed by Francis Bacon in the *Advancement of Learning*. When he sold this library to Congress in 1815, thus providing the nucleus of the modern-day Library of Congress, his collection numbered nearly 6,500 volumes and required ten wagons to transport from Charlottesville to Washington. By the time of his death in 1826, he had again collected nearly a thousand volumes. These books he hoped might form the basis of the library of the university he was then founding in Charlottesville, but upon Jefferson's death his executor was forced to sell the collection to pay off a portion of the indebtedness of Jefferson's estate.

Jefferson's love of books was far more than that of a mere collector, however. He read deeply and widely in classical as well as contemporary literature. While he thought the speculations of Plato to be "unintelligible jargon" and the fountainhead of meaningless mysticism, he held in high admiration the writings of other classical authors who enlarged his understanding of moral philosophy, politics, and history of the Western world. And, although he considered much of modern fiction to be a mere "mass of trash," he concluded that there were at least a few novelists and poets of more recent times whose writings might serve as "useful vehicles of a sound morality."[16]

Perhaps most significantly, however, Jefferson considered Francis Bacon, Isaac Newton, and John Locke to be the greatest trinity of thinkers that had ever lived. These architects of the Enlightenment were in the vanguard of a cadre of mentors who connected the classical world to the modern world of the eighteenth century. They were foremost among those who nurtured the scientific, rationalistic, and optimistic outlook that shaped his thought and directed his energies. They were, as historian Henry May emphasized, above all else, useful—"useful as guides for the moral conduct of life and the construction of a republican polity."[17]

Singularly important among the Enlightenment doctrines that came to be shared by Jefferson and his circle was the conviction that the universe itself was entirely rational and lawful and that critical thought and untrammeled inquiry would enable people to expose whatever was false or harmful in human affairs. Jefferson believed that the world was controlled, in all its manifestations, by the laws of nature established by the Divine Creator. He held that people could use their reason to understand the workings of the universe and, even more importantly, discover those universal laws "engraved on our hearts." In Jeffersonian political theory, the nature of government was defined by and dependent upon the nature of mankind. Thus, it was ultimately "the Laws of Nature and of Nature's God" operative in humanity that he believed must set the standards and bounds of civil society and make possible a government dedicated to the honor and preservation of those principles.[18]

Taking his cue from John Locke, Jefferson's acceptance of the doctrine of natural rights led him to maintain that government was instituted among men by consent and that the rights with which they were endowed by their Creator must not be usurped by government in any form. In his *Summary View of the Rights of British America*, which predated the Declaration of Independence by two years, Jefferson unequivocally stated his position: "The God who gave us life gave us liberty at the same time: the hand of force may destroy, but cannot disjoin them." The role of the government, the agent of the people, was therefore clear and limited. It was to secure and protect the citizenry's natural and inalienable rights—those rights that are above temporal law, above history. Jefferson's insistence that these God-given rights be recognized and respected led him to oppose adoption of the Constitution until the addition of an explicit Bill of Rights was assured.[19]

Believing that people were, on the whole, rational, moral, and benevolent social creatures, Jefferson agreed with the dictum that government should be conducted by the will of the majority. However, he held as a "sacred principle" the maxim that majority will, to be just, must be reasonable and cognizant of the fact that "the minority possess their equal rights, which equal laws must protect …." It was his belief in mankind's God-given moral sense and rationality that enabled Jefferson to declare that error of opinion can be tolerated as long as reason is left free to combat it and that, in a properly constituted—and enlightened— republican society, the people themselves are the best and surest guardians of their liberties.[20]

In Jefferson's mind, the very survival of the ideal of republican citizenship depended upon the spread of knowledge among the people. Thus, to Jefferson, educational theory was inseparable from political theory. Whenever Jefferson looked to education in any form, he did so with the eye of a statesman concerned with the welfare and rights of the citizenry. Conversely, in his political activities and writings, he was often self-consciously the master educator, striving to give clear definition and meaning to the ideals of a free and just society. Nowhere is this more apparent than in the sharp and forceful language he used to announce to the world the rights of a free people: "We hold these truths to be self-evident: that all men are created equal; that they are endowed by their Creator with certain inalienable rights; that among these are life, liberty and the pursuit of happiness; that to secure these rights, governments are instituted among men, deriving their just powers from the consent of the governed; that whenever any form of government becomes destructive of these ends, it is the right of the people to alter or abolish it, and to institute new government, laying its foundations on such principles, and organizing its powers in such form, as to them shall seem most likely to effect their safety and happiness."[21]

It is in this declaration that we find both the basis of Jefferson's political belief and his rationale for the necessity of an enlightened society. Fifty years after he heralded the rights of a free people and enumerated the long train of abuses that he maintained justified revolution, Jefferson reflected on the universal power and appeal of the Declaration. "May it," he wrote with a feeble hand at the age of eighty-three, "be to the world, what I believe it will be (to some parts sooner, to others later, but finally to all), the signal of arousing men to burst the chains under which monkish ignorance and superstition had persuaded them to bind themselves, and to assume the blessings of liberty and security of self-government." In this same letter, which was to be the last he would ever write, Jefferson asserted his bold belief that: "All eyes are opened, or opening, to the rights of man." The general spread of knowledge, he wrote, "has already laid open to every view the palpable truth, that the mass of mankind has not been born with saddles on their backs, nor a favored few booted and spurred, ready to ride them legitimately, by the grace of God. These are grounds of hope for others."

For some who lived in the Age of Jefferson and beyond—most notably African Americans, both those enslaved and free, Native Americans, and women —the "grounds of hope" proved to be a long-delayed promise, yet as Abraham Lincoln and Martin Luther King, Jr., both stressed in later ages, Jefferson's words proved to be prophetic. Although Jefferson's own actions did not always accord with his political theory and moral philosophy, in his public papers and in the tens of thousands of letters that have survived, the essential elements of his convictions unmistakably shine through. Dumas Malone, the premier biographer of Jefferson, noted that the best single clue to Jefferson's motives in the Revolution and throughout his entire career was his concern for "the attainment and maintenance of liberty." If Jefferson could expediently adjust his methods to meet particular problems and on more than one occasion acted on his belief that what is practical must sometimes control what is theoretically proper, he nonetheless remained constant in his devotion to the cause of asserting and advocating humanity's inalienable rights. Throughout his life he persistently proclaimed the doctrines to which he had given classic form in the Declaration of Independence, and in his last years he could still fervently affirm: "Nothing … is unchangeable but the inherent and unalienable rights of man."[22]

DOCUMENTS

ON THE SUBJECT OF A

SYSTEM OF PUBLIC EDUCATION,

FOR THE STATE OF VIRGINIA.

A BILL *for the more general diffusion of Knowledge, proposed by the Committee of Revisors of the Laws of Virginia, appointed by the General Assembly in the year 1776.*

SECTION 1. WHEREAS it appeareth, that however certain forms of government are better calculated than others to protect individuals in the free exercise of their natural rights, and are at the same time themselves better guarded against degeneracy, yet experience hath shewn, that, even under the best forms, those entrusted with power have, in time, and by slow operations, perverted it into tyranny; and it is believed that the most effectual means of preventing this would be to illuminate, as far as practicable, the minds of the people at large, and more especially to give them knowledge of those facts which history exhibiteth, that, possessed thereby of the experience of other ages and countries, they may be enabled to know ambition under all its shapes, and prompt to exert their natural powers to defeat its purposes; and whereas it is generally true that that people will be happiest whose laws are best, and are best administered, and that laws will be wisely formed, and honestly administered, in proportion as those who form and administer them are wise and honest; whence it becomes expedient for promoting the public happiness that those persons, whom nature hath endowed with genius and virtue, should be rendered by liberal education worthy to receive, and able to guard, the sacred deposit of the rights and liberties of

First page of an 1817 reprinting of Jefferson's 1779 Bill for the General Diffusion of Knowledge. (Courtesy The Library of Virginia)

Chapter Three

THE EDUCATION OF REPUBLICAN CITIZENS

It is an axiom in my mind that our liberty can never be safe but in the hands of the people themselves, and that too of the people with a certain degree of instruction. This it is the business of the state to effect, and on a general plan.

— THOMAS JEFFERSON TO GEORGE
WASHINGTON, JANUARY 4, 1786[23]

The two most famous of Thomas Jefferson's early political writings, A Summary View of the Rights of British America and the Declaration of Independence, were in spirit and substance educational as well as political treatises. Jefferson himself testified to the educative role of the Declaration by asserting that his aim was: "… [N]ot to find out new principles, or new arguments, never before thought of, not merely to say things which have never been said before; but to place before mankind the common sense of the subject, in terms so plain and firm as to command their assent, and to justify ourselves in the independent stand we are compelled to take. Neither aiming at originality of principle or sentiment, nor yet copied from any particular previous writing, it was intended to be an expression of the American mind, and to give to that expression the proper tone and spirit called for by the occasion."[24]

No matter how plain the language or rational the principles, however, Jefferson realized that the message of the Declaration would be comprehended only slowly by others, whether in his own or future generations, and on either side of the Atlantic. Neither proclamations nor wars could guarantee the survival of a nation founded on lofty ideas, no matter how carefully the words might be crafted or how bravely its citizen soldiers might engage enemy troops. Thus, at the conclusion of his momentous work in Philadelphia in the summer of 1776, Jefferson promptly returned to Virginia, there to undertake the first meaningful steps toward making the promises of the Declaration a reality. Upon taking his seat as a member of the state legislature, Jefferson immediately immersed himself in the practical business of translating abstract principles into laws and institutions that would safeguard them for posterity.

Convinced that the entire legal legacy inherited from the past must be reviewed "with a single eye to reason and the good of those for whose government it was framed," Jefferson in the fall of 1776 proposed with a sense of urgency the creation of a special committee to undertake a study and revision of the laws of the Commonwealth of Virginia. This committee, consisting initially of Edmund Pendleton, George Wythe, George Mason, Thomas Ludwell Lee, and Jefferson, met at Fredericksburg on January 13, 1777, to decide upon the scope of their task and division of assignments. Considering but then rejecting as too extreme the notion of abolishing all existing laws and attempting to replace them with an entirely new legal code, the group apportioned among themselves the work of reconsidering and revising as necessary extant British statutes as well as laws that had been adopted while Virginia had been a colonial entity. Mason, not being a lawyer, begged to be excused from the committee, as did Lee, who then died shortly afterwards. Jefferson picked up the bulk of the work initially assigned to these men and, with his co-laborers Wythe and Pendleton, undertook a work that aimed at nothing less than the reformation—indeed, the transformation—of the newly proclaimed republican society.[25]

Working independently for over two years and then coming together at Williamsburg to compare notes, iron out differences, and eventually reach agreement on the proper wording of their proposed legislative measures, this trio of distinguished lawyers produced 126 bills for the consideration of the Virginia General Assembly. With Jefferson in the lead, their project had been to draft legislation designed to eradicate long-accepted vestiges of privilege and injustice and to lay the foundation for a truly republican form of government. It was during this period that Jefferson introduced bills to abolish entails and primogeniture, reform courts of justice, and make more rational and humane the system of punishments for crimes. In a separate document, intended by Jefferson to be a constitution for the state of Virginia, he proposed providing grants of land and thus extending the franchise to all citizens. His draft constitution was rejected as were many of the proposals submitted by the revisers, such as the bill, drafted by Jefferson, that provided for the gradual emancipation of slaves. Some of the bills for which Jefferson was responsible, directly or indirectly, passed only after years of debate and sometimes in severely modified form. That the legislature eventually passed fewer than half of the 126 bills proposed by the committee underscores the political and psychic barriers separating Jefferson and his legal compatriots from the planters in whose midst they lived and on whose votes their measures depended.[26]

Among the bills that did survive and that erected a fundamental protection of freedom of belief and worship was Bill 82 that became the Virginia Statute for Religious Freedom. Jefferson later prized this act, which disestablished the Anglican Church in Virginia, as second only to the Declaration of Independence as his most significant contribution to the freedom of mankind. It declared that no one could be compelled to attend church or be made to support any religion not of his own choosing; that no one could be made to suffer reprisals for belief or nonbelief in religion; that, in sum, "all men shall be free to profess, and by argument to maintain, their opinions in matters of religion, and that the same shall in no wise diminish, enlarge, or affect their civil capacities." As Jefferson endeavored to explain a few years after the bill's adoption, "The legitimate powers of government extend to such acts only as are injurious to others." He then added: "But it does me no injury for my neighbor to say there are twenty gods, or no god. It neither picks my pocket nor breaks my leg." While there were certainly many who agreed with Jefferson's defense of separation of church and state, his later observation probably engendered more criticism of Jefferson than anything else he said or did during his entire lifetime. It was, nonetheless, a basic tenet of his belief and reflected a fundamental principle on which his famous statute rested.[27]

Although proud of this achievement and believing it to be important, at that time Jefferson considered Bill 79, The Bill for the General Diffusion of Knowledge, to be "*the most important bill*" in the entire legislative package that the committee submitted in printed form to the legislature on June 18, 1779. Drafted by Jefferson in the fall of 1778, this bill, like that which provided for religious liberty, was intended as yet another blow against the traditions that limited intellectual freedom. And, as with the bills that abolished the practices of entails and primogeniture, the Bill for the More General Diffusion of Knowledge, had it passed in the form Jefferson devised and proved effective in practice, might have had some effect in enhancing social mobility by increasing educational opportunity. "Worth and genius would thus have been sought out from every condition of life," Jefferson wrote in later years to John Adams, "and [would have been] completely prepared by education for defeating the competition of wealth and birth for public trusts." Most importantly, Jefferson hoped the establishment of a system of publicly supported schools would elevate the mass of people to the moral status necessary to insure good government and public safety and happiness. To Jefferson, the survival of all the freedoms being declared and fought for in the Revolution ultimately depended less on the outcome of battles than on the enlightenment of the people.[28]

In the preamble to Jefferson's education bill, he reminded his legislative colleagues that experience had shown that, even under the best forms of government, "those entrusted with power have, in time, and by slow operations, perverted it into tyranny." The most effective safeguard against this tendency, Jefferson asserted, would be "to illuminate, as far as practicable, the minds of the people at large" by providing for a proper system of education. Rejecting the conventional wisdom of the day, Jefferson noted further that it was not sufficient merely to allow those born into privileged families to obtain an education. The indigence of the majority of the population was such, he argued, that many children "whom nature hath fitly formed and disposed to become useful instruments for the public" have no opportunity for education and thus being of service to society. Jefferson's proposal, so simple to our ears, ran completely counter to the prevailing laissez-faire custom. It is better, he maintained, that all should be educated "at the common expense of all, than that the happiness of all should be confided to the weak or wicked."[29]

The general outlines of Jefferson's bill are familiar, although in the context of eighteenth-century Virginia, the provisions he articulated were quite novel.

Jefferson proposed that each county elect three aldermen whose first task would be to subdivide the county into wards, or "hundreds," of sufficient size to support a school that could be attended daily by the children of that vicinity. In addition to determining the most convenient location for and supervising the erection of a school house in each ward, the aldermen were to be charged with the responsibility of selecting an "overseer" for every ten or so schools. These overseers would have the duty of appointing teachers, inspecting the schools, examining the pupils periodically, and insuring that the course of instruction was approved by the Board of Visitors, or governing body, of the College of William and Mary. The maintenance of the schools and salaries of the teachers, along with their board, lodging, and laundry, would be provided by county funds.

Reading, writing, and arithmetic were specified by Jefferson as the principal subjects to be taught in these primary or elementary schools, with special attention to be given to books that would instruct in ancient and modern history. Instead of drawing moral lessons from the Bible, which Jefferson thought beyond the comprehension of young children, he contended that the histories of Greece, Rome, Europe, and America contained abundant examples of aggressive and abusive behavior by both men and nations that would enable citizens to recognize and thus prevent the reappearance of injustice and tyranny. History, by informing students of the past, would "qualify them as judges of the actions and designs of men" and thus would "enable them to know ambition under every disguise it may assume; and knowing it, to defeat its views."[30]

In his zeal to diffuse knowledge generally among the citizenry, Jefferson was perhaps overly confident about the learning abilities of children. As Jefferson scholar Merrill Peterson observed, European thinkers such as Jean Jacques Rousseau and Johann Pestalozzi were already challenging the rationalistic and formalistic approach to education assumed appropriate by Jefferson. But Jefferson was less concerned with the methods of pedagogy than with purpose and system. His primary concern was to create convenient and adequately supported schools that would provide the general population with the skills and understandings necessary to perform their duties and protect their rights as citizens.[31]

If in pedagogy Jefferson was conventional, he was hardly so in the comprehensiveness of his plan or in his call for public support of the schools he was proposing be erected throughout the state. On a small scale the principle of public education was not untried. For several generations certain New England communities had endeavored, with uneven success, to maintain common schools supported by local communities. In addition, William Smith, a friend of Benjamin Franklin and an advocate of education in New York and Philadelphia, had proposed publicly sponsored elementary instruction in his 1753 utopian tract, *A General Idea of the College of Mirania.* But Virginia, which at the time included the present states of West Virginia, Kentucky and the great expanse of territory beyond the Ohio River, was hardly on the order of a New England commonwealth—and certainly was far from being a utopian society. Thus, well in advance of the period when Horace Mann, Henry Barnard, and other fathers of the common school movement began their crusade for state organized and publicly funded school systems, Jefferson was proposing that his state undertake its own crusade against

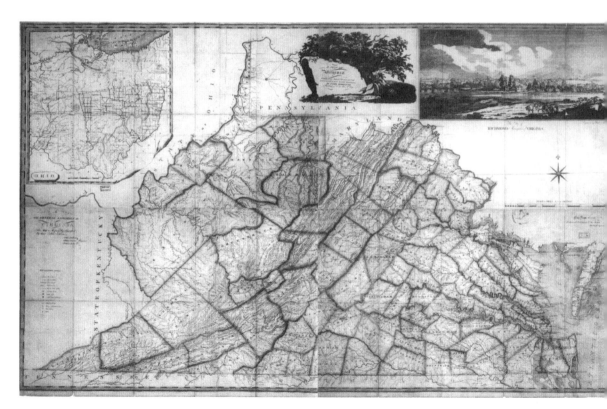

A Map of Virginia *(1807) by Bishop James Madison. (Courtesy Library of Congress)*

ignorance. To insure that even the poorest citizens would have access to these schools, Jefferson specified that "all the free children, male and female, resident with the respective hundred, shall be entitled to receive tuition gratis, for a term of three years, and as much longer, at their private expense, as their parents, guardians or friends, shall think proper." Provision for the free education of all citizens, according to Jefferson's plan, would establish the foundation upon which the rest of a unified pyramidal system of education could be erected.[32]

In addition to providing a general education for the masses, Jefferson insisted that the state had an equal obligation to seek out and cultivate leaders, members of the natural aristocracy. It was expedient, he reasoned, that for the promotion of public happiness, "those persons, whom nature hath endowed with genius and virtue, should be rendered by liberal education worthy to receive, and able to guard the sacred deposit of the rights and liberties of their fellow citizens ...." He thus proposed that, with public funds made available by the state treasurer, twenty grammar or secondary schools be fixed at appropriate geographical locations throughout the state. As boarding schools, these brick or stone structures were to contain "a room for the school, a hall to dine in, four rooms for a master and usher, and ten or twelve lodging rooms for the scholars." These specifications, as well as the provision that one hundred acres of land be set aside by the commonwealth for the use and support of each boarding school, signify that these institutions, not unlike the pavilions or faculty residences with attached student rooms he later designed for the University of Virginia, were envisioned by Jefferson to be impressive as well as permanent features of his overall education plan.[33]

As for the curriculum at this secondary level, Jefferson noted that in addition to the traditional focus on Latin and Greek, these schools also were to incorporate English grammar, geography, and some advanced branches of mathematics. Perhaps of more importance, however, was Jefferson's provision for the continuing education of those boys whose performance in the elementary schools had shown them to be the most able and promising students in each district. Each year, based on "the most diligent and impartial examination and enquiry," one boy, whose parents could not afford to pay for additional education, was to be selected annually to receive a scholarship to cover room, board, and tuition for further education in a grammar school. After this additional year of schooling, one-third of this group would be discontinued as "public foundationers;" after the second year, all the rest would be discontinued as scholarship students "save one only, the best in genius and disposition" in each secondary school. This student, the presumed valedictorian in each of the grammar schools, would continue his education free of charge for four more years. These scholarship boys in each successive class would study side by side with the sons of parents who could afford to pay tuition for this more advanced level of education. "By this means," Jefferson noted, "twenty of the best geniuses will be raked from the rubbish annually, and be instructed, at the public expense, so far as the grammar schools go."[34]

Jefferson's hierarchical scheme as outlined in his Bill for the More General Diffusion of Knowledge contained yet another feature designed to provide the most outstanding secondary school graduates with scholarships to attend the College of William and Mary. As specified in his 1779 plan, in every even-numbered year the visitors representing the district schools south and west of the James River would select "one among the said seniors, of the best learning and most hopeful genius and disposition" to proceed to the College of William and Mary. In odd-numbered years a student residing north and east of the James would be similarly selected. By this scheme, only one student per year would be given a scholarship for three additional years of collegiate study at William and Mary.

However, in his *Notes on the State of Virginia*, written just a few years after the original bill was drafted, Jefferson indicated that ten students a year might have been granted college scholarships. In *Notes* he stated that, of the twenty gifted students who completed the grammar schools at state expense each year, "one half are to be discontinued (from among whom the grammar schools will probably be supplied with future masters); and the other half, who are to be chosen for the superiority of their parts and disposition, are to be sent and continued three years in the study of such sciences as they shall choose, at William and Mary College." In his *Notes* he summarized the intended result of his plan by observing that, in addition to providing all children in the state with the essentials of reading, writing, and arithmetic, "ten annually of superior genius, well taught in Greek, Latin, geography and the higher branches of arithmetic" would be produced and "ten others, annually, of still superior parts, who, to those branches of learning, shall have added such of the sciences as their genius shall have led them to ...." [35]

Whether at this stage of his thinking Jefferson intended for only one or perhaps as many as ten boys per year to receive scholarships to William and Mary is unclear, but Jefferson was totally clear and definite about the general object of the law: "to provide an education adapted to the years, to the capacity, and the condition of every one, and directed to their freedom and happiness." Jefferson's imprecision regarding the number of collegiate scholarships might be excused (although not settled) by his statement in the *Notes* that "Specific details were not proper for the law," but no doubt awareness of legislative resistance to the expense of the entire undertaking motivated him to look for ways to economize and may explain in part this inconsistency. [36]

By placing more emphasis by way of detail on the establishment of schools for the general population than on the particulars of higher education in Bill 79, Jefferson was by no means discounting the importance of educating a leadership cadre. Two companion bills need to be understood as extensions of the Bill for the General Diffusion of Knowledge. Bill 80, A Bill for Amending the Constitution of the College of William and Mary, was intended to convert Jefferson's staid alma mater into a public university of the highest grade and place it on more secure financial standing. Bill 81, A Bill for Establishing a Public Library, was not, as its title might imply, designed to create a library for the general reading public (although Jefferson later proposed circulating libraries for every county), but rather had as its purpose the establishment of a research institution for the use of "the learned and curious" so that scholars, public officials, and citizens of superior talent could extend their knowledge to the highest levels. [37]

Jefferson had long despaired of the lack of public purpose of William and Mary, a college that, in spite of receiving some public revenues through the years, was considered an establishment of the Church of England. Jefferson noted that the College's visitors "were required to be all of that Church; the Professors to subscribe to its thirty-nine Articles; its Students to learn its Catechism; and one of its fundamental objects was declared to be, to raise up Ministers for that church." In Bill 80, Jefferson proposed amending the College's charter so as to "render the institution publicly advantageous." Among the measures he advocated was the replacement of the self-perpetuating governing board of Anglicans with a secular board appointed annually by the legislature. The number of professorships was to be enlarged from six to eight with increased emphasis on "the laws of nature and of nations," fine arts, government and history, anatomy and medicine, mathematics, physical and natural sciences, and modern as well as classical languages. Jefferson proposed that the Indian School long associated with the college be made to shift its focus from that of teaching Indian boys the three Rs and the principles of Christianity to the larger task of investigating the laws, customs, religions, tradi-tions, and languages of the various Indian tribes and to amassing a collection of their grammars, vocabularies, and other materials that could be preserved and studied.

Jefferson was unambiguous with regard to his intentions pertaining to the reform of William and Mary. In his Autobiography he stated that the amend-ments to the college's constitution were needed in order to "to enlarge its sphere of science, and to make it in fact a University." If some Anglicans resisted Jefferson's proposed reforms because of their opposition to the secularization and moderniza-tion of their college, some other Virginians, members of dissenting sects, perhaps feared that Jefferson's bill might actually strengthen the influence of the Anglican sect. This latter explanation was offered by Jefferson as one reason, at least, that this bill, like the bill for establishing a public library in Richmond, died in legislative committee.[38]

When Jefferson was elected governor of the state in 1779, he was able to bring about at least some reforms at William and Mary. He succeeded in replacing three of the existing professorships (in divinity, oriental languages, and Greek and Latin) with professorships in law and government, anatomy and medicine, and modern languages. Greek and Latin were still to be taught, but in the grammar school, not the collegiate department. He managed also to convert the Indian school into a kind of anthropological chair for the study of American Indians. These measures fell far short of Jefferson's more ambitious designs for establishing a university, however, and with the demise of his reform bill, he basically abandoned all hope of making significant changes in the oldest college in the state. In the future, he would push for a new university based on constitutional and curricular principles notably different from any existing college or university in the country.[39]

Jefferson's general education bill, like the bills to reform William and Mary and to establish a research library in the state's capital, also met with defeat. Bill 79 received an encouraging reception when first brought before the House of Delegates in December 1778 and after several readings and some amending, was actually passed by that body in December of 1785. However, the bill died in the Senate.

At the time of the final debates surrounding the bill, Jefferson was unable to be present as its advocate. During this time, 1784-1789, he was residing in Paris while serving as the American Minister to France. Separated by an ocean from the deliberations that would determine the fate of his "most important bill," he nonetheless tried to use all the influence he could to secure the bill's passage. In letters to Washington, Madison, Wythe, and others, Jefferson eloquently pleaded in behalf of his education measure. Surely expecting his friends to share his words with others, he reminded his correspondents of the vital connection between liberty and the diffusion of knowledge, asserting that "no other sure foundation can be devised for the preservation of freedom and happiness." In an oft-quoted passage in which Jefferson compared the unhappy masses of Europe with the common citizens of America, he implored his mentor and friend George Wythe to: "Preach, my dear Sir, a crusade against ignorance; establish and improve law for educating the common people. Let our countrymen know that the people alone can protect us against these evils [the misery caused by kings, nobles, and priests] and that the tax which will be paid for this purpose is not more than the thousandth part of what will be paid to kings, priests and nobles who will rise up among us if we leave the people in ignorance."[40]

Jefferson's pleadings and the political maneuverings of Wythe, Madison, and other allies in the General Assembly proved unable to turn the tide in favor of Jefferson's education bill. After one last attempt to have the bill considered favorably in 1786, Madison reluctantly wrote to Jefferson that the expense of the undertaking, along with concerns raised regarding the sparse population density in some sections of the state, were the primary barriers to its passage. Madison expressed the hope that some future legislature might be more successful in terms of putting the bill "into some shape that will lessen the objection of expense." Disappointed but not yet defeated, Jefferson some months later responded to Madison: "Above all things I hope the education of the common people will be attended to; convinced that on their good sense we may rely with the most security for the preservation of a due degree of liberty."[41]

Madison's hope that a later legislature might prove wiser than those of the 1780s proved to be wishful thinking as far as Jefferson's general education bill was concerned. When the bill resurfaced again in 1796, the result was equally disappointing. Although the Assembly passed an Act to Establish Public Schools in 1796 that retained some of the phraseology of Jefferson's 1779 bill, especially that providing for the election of aldermen, the act provided only for primary schools *if* and *when* local court officials deemed it feasible to provide for them. This permissive provision of the statute weakened the measure beyond recognition. Jefferson later noted that since the law provided that the cost of maintaining the schools should be apportioned on the basis of wealth, "the justices, being generally of the more wealthy class, were unwilling to incur that burden." Jefferson could not recall a single county in the state that initiated local public schools as a result of this law. In Jefferson's view, his bill had been "completely defeated."[42]

It is easy enough in the long perspective of history to find flaws in Jefferson's scheme. For all of his concern for the equalization of opportunity, his proposal still left the children of the wealthy with a clear advantage over those of less fortunate circumstances. Those who could pay tuition need not stand the periodic examinations and run the risk of being weeded out; only the "public" students had to face such hurdles. In a sense then, Jefferson's proposal represented a modest compromise between public and private education. The advantages of birth and wealth remained, although now Jefferson was proposing that the children of the common folk be at least allowed to enter the contest.

It might also be objected that the very restrictions Jefferson placed on the upward flow of students were overly competitive and "elitist." Jefferson was an advocate of meritocracy long before that term was coined, but it seems unjust to charge him with the motive of seeking to create a privileged elite, even a natural one. Jefferson's belief that citizens of superior talents were "the most precious gift of nature for the instruction, the trusts, and the government of society" was not in his mind at all antithetical to his belief that "Every government degenerates when trusted to the rulers of the people alone." His object was not to create classes of the rulers and the ruled, but by providing opportunity for all to progress as far as their natures allowed, to render the people themselves "safe as they are the ultimate guardians of their own liberty." As it was, even this modest proposal to extend educational opportunity was seen as radical in the context of eighteenth-century Virginia. Not only was his plan a direct strike against the aristocracy of birth and wealth, but his suggestion that the schools be maintained by public taxation placed the heaviest burden upon the very people who might indeed question why they should be asked to pay for the education of the poor, regardless of their talent.[43]

Jefferson, of course, had repeatedly tried to answer that question and continued to do so in years to come. His labors on behalf of the general spread of knowledge did not end with the defeat of the three education proposals he introduced to the Virginia legislature during the struggle for independence. Jefferson returned to the fray in diverse ways as the demands of service to his expanding country drew him ever more prominently onto the national stage and more deeply into political controversy. Even while active as secretary of state under George Washington, vice president under John Adams, and president himself from 1801 through 1809, Jefferson monitored and encouraged educational developments and ideas at home and abroad. On several occasions during the years when Jefferson was separated from Virginia for long periods of time, he emerged to champion educational causes that gave promise of fulfilling, at least in part, his expanding vision of the forms of education needed by a people in pursuit of freedom and happiness.

Chapter Four

EDUCATION AND THE CONTINUING AMERICAN REVOLUTION

The generation which commences a revolution can rarely complete it.
Habituated from their infancy to passive submission of body and mind to
their kings and priests, they are not qualified, when called on, to think and
provide for themselves ... [but] ... as a younger and more instructed race
comes on ... one of the ever renewed attempts will ultimately succeed.

— THOMAS JEFFERSON TO JOHN ADAMS,
SEPTEMBER 4, 1823[44]

While serving as minister to France in 1785, Thomas Jefferson received a letter from John Banister, Jr., a Virginian then making the grand tour, seeking his advice regarding "the best seminary for the education of youth in Europe." Jefferson dutifully replied with commentary on the relative merits of Geneva and Rome, which at the time he considered the most desirable European centers of learning. Rather abruptly, however, Jefferson then diverted his correspondent's attention to a more fundamental question: "But why send an American youth to Europe for education?"[45]

Jefferson's question was far from rhetorical. He both respected and resented Europe's claims of superiority in cultural matters. He had undertaken his mission to France with some concern that he might himself be perceived as "a savage from the mountains of America." He found himself dazzled and charmed by the gracious manners and refinement of the French elite, and yet was appalled at the misery and squalor that he observed among the masses in France. "The general fate of humanity here [is] most deplorable," he instructed young Banister, noting that "the great mass of people are suffering under physical and moral oppression." Jefferson contended that even among the aristocracy there was less happiness and domestic tranquility in France than was enjoyed by the general population in America. Jefferson's experiences in Europe as well as his study of history prompted him to give thanks repeatedly for the fact that a great ocean separated the fledgling American republic from the contamination of European conditions and conventions.[46]

In light of Jefferson's ambivalent assessment of European society, it is not surprising that, in his reply to Banister, he was brief not only in his treatment of the question regarding the best seat of learning in the Old World, but also in his mention of the studies he thought most appropriate for youth in the New World. He recommended knowledge of the classical and modern languages, especially French, Spanish, and Italian. He also listed mathematics, chemistry, agriculture, botany, and other branches of science, as well as the study of history and ethics. Studies such as these Jefferson considered the bare essentials, the core areas of knowledge that should be in the possession of any American who sought enlightenment.

In numerous other letters and documents written both before and after his exchange with Banister, Jefferson elaborated in some detail on the value of these and other fields of study. In this letter, however, he deemed a mere listing to be sufficient. Jefferson in this instance was intent on engaging an issue that he considered more pressing than that of the textual substance or content of education. The value or usefulness of education, Jefferson reasoned here, is determined by context as well as by content. To Jefferson, the kind of education most valuable for republican citizens was one that could be acquired more surely and more safely in the raw towns and villages of the new American nation than in the ancient and revered capitals of Europe. An American abroad, educated as a foreigner in terms of his affections, values, tastes, and even in style and manner of writing and speaking, Jefferson warned, would become alienated and lost. To drive his point home, Jefferson appealed to Banister's own experience as an American: "Cast your eye over America: who are the men of most learning, of most eloquence, most beloved by their countrymen and most trusted by them? They are those who have been educated among them, and whose manners, morals, and habits, are perfectly homogeneous with those of the country."[47]

However, Jefferson's growing nationalistic pride could not conceal the fact that he was increasingly frustrated with the slow advance of education in both Virginia and throughout the nation. While his letter to Banister was an appeal to a rising American consciousness, Jefferson was painfully aware of American shortcomings in the educational sphere. When in 1788 Ralph Izard, a prominent South Carolinian, solicited Jefferson's advice regarding his younger son's desire to become an engineer, Jefferson had to confess to American deficiency. He sent Izard information on two French institutions that far outdistanced any institution in the United States in terms of offerings in applied mathematics, mechanics, physics, and other sciences essential to engineering studies. If the ideal situation was to provide Americans with instruction in "every branch of science, useful at this day ... taught in its highest degree," as Jefferson devoutly wished, then his country-men had to face and overcome obvious deficiencies.[48]

Jefferson's desire to elevate the level of learning available in the United States, especially in terms of the useful sciences, prompted him to consider a number of schemes, both foreign and domestic in origin, in the years before as well as during his presidency. One rather interesting proposal that caught Jefferson's attention, at least for a brief moment around the time his own educational proposals were sinking, was the grandiose plan of a Frenchman, Quesnay de Beaurepaire. The grand-son of Louis XV's personal physician, Quesnay had been an engineering captain in the American army under Lafayette's command and for a short time after the close of the war operated a school in Richmond before returning to France. In the mid-1780s Quesnay determined to establish on the site of his former school an Academy of Arts and Sciences patterned after the famous French Academy. Complementing the institution in Richmond were to be branches in Baltimore, Philadelphia, and New York, all of which were to be affiliated with the royal soci-eties of London, Paris, Brussels, and other learned bodies of Europe. Under the tutelage of French professors and with the additional support of 175 non-resident associates, including Jefferson, students were to receive instruction in specialized academic schools and were to conduct investigations in a wide array of academic fields. The list of studies outlined by Quesnay included foreign languages, mathematics, physics, design, architecture, painting, sculpture, astronomy, geography, chemistry, botany, anatomy, and natural history. Scientific experts dispatched from Paris would not only offer instruction to students, but would advise government commissions, corporations, and stock companies regarding investments in the hitherto unknown and unexploited resources of the country. There was little that might be accounted modest about Quesnay's plan.[49]

After returning to France, Quesnay most likely discussed his idea with Jefferson who at the time was residing in Paris as minister to the court of Versailles. Apparently encouraged by Jefferson, Quesnay listed Jefferson as a sponsor in his prospectus for the academy, along with Lafayette, Beaumarchais, Condorcet, Lavoisier, Houdon, and numerous other French and American celebrities. Quesnay managed to raise a considerable amount of money as well as moral support on both sides of the Atlantic for the venture. The cornerstone for the Richmond Academy was laid on June 24, 1786, with great fanfare, but the outbreak of the French Revolution three years later brought an abrupt end to the elaborate scheme before the new building could be put to its intended use. Even before the events following the storming of the Bastille doomed Quesnay's project, however, Jefferson had pulled back from whatever initial support he may have given. Determining that there would be little legislative support for the undertaking, and suggesting that European professors might be disappointed in their expectations of America, Jefferson cautioned Quesnay on January 6, 1788, that he feared the project was "too extensive for the poverty of the country." While he claimed to wish Quesnay "every possible success" and said that he would "be really happy to see the plan answer your expectations," his expressed desire to remain "absolutely neutral" concerning the future of the project clearly revealed that he had deep reservations.[50]

However conflicted Jefferson may have been regarding his reluctance to push Quesnay's plan, his reaction a few years later to a proposal from a professor at the University of Geneva, Francois D'Ivernois, was quite different. D'Ivernois, described by Jefferson as a man of "considerable distinction for science and patriotism, and that too of the republican kind," informed Jefferson in 1794 that the faculty of the University of Geneva had become dissatisfied with their political environment and would consider transplanting themselves to the United States if proper arrangements could be made. Excited by the prospect of luring the faculty of such an esteemed institution to Virginia, Jefferson asked Wilson Cary Nicholas to gauge, quietly, the sentiments of key members of the state legislature regarding their stance on this proposition. However, based on information later provided by Nicholas, Jefferson once again had his high hopes dashed by opposition from the Virginia legislature.

Nicholas informed Jefferson that although there was some support for the project, the majority of the legislators could not be persuaded to back the measure. In informing D'Ivernois of his disappointment, Jefferson listed three reasons that seemed to render the scheme unworkable: American students would have difficulty with instruction conveyed in the French language, the population base was insufficient to warrant and sustain such an institution, and long-term financial support could not be guaranteed. Jefferson explained to D'Ivernois that the short-sighted decision rested with others and that he personally would have been delighted to have such an institution established in Virginia. Moreover, Jefferson assured D'Ivernois that his own devotion to "science, and freedom, the first-born daughter of science" was so firm that he would have been tempted to establish a second residence in whatever neighborhood the institution might have been placed.[51]

Not yet submitting to defeat, Jefferson sought President George Washington's support for the idea. Knowing that Washington had a long-standing interest in seeing a national university established in the Federal City, Jefferson proposed that Washington throw his support, financial and personal, behind the Geneva project. Within weeks after having sent his letter of regret to D'Ivernois, Jefferson wrote to Washington with the suggestion that the president donate his shares of stock in the Potomac and James River canal companies to underwrite the transfer of the Geneva professors to America. Governor Patrick Henry and the Virginia legislature had presented Washington with the stock in 1785 as a gift in recognition of his heroic service to the state and nation. Embarrassed over the appearance of profiting from his service, Washington previously had solicited advice from Jefferson and others as to the best way to dispose of the stock gift that might in some way advance education in the state.

As Jefferson described the plan to Washington, the Geneva faculty could become the nucleus of a national university, a university that could be located *near* the capital but *within* the borders of Virginia since that state would be contributing to its support by paying interest on the donated stock. This national university, Jefferson assured Washington, would draw students "from all our states" and probably from other parts of the hemisphere as well. Washington, however, had already been informed of the proposal by John Adams, who had also been contacted by D'Ivernois. Washington replied to Jefferson that he was not enthusiastic about the idea. The president noted that it might not be wise to transplant the Geneva professors *en masse* because they "might not all be good characters nor all sufficiently acquainted with our language." Moreover, said Washington, their political principles seemed at variance with the democratic movement in their own country and might give further support to those who, "without any just cause that I can discover, are continually sounding the bell of aristocracy." Washington also thought it better, if foreign professors were to be attracted to this country, to draw them from several nations rather than all from one. Lacking neither the support of the Virginia legislature nor that of the president of the United States, Jefferson abandoned this project that initially he had embraced with far more enthusiasm than he had Quesnay's earlier proposal.[52]

As vice president of the United States during the administration of John Adams, Jefferson served in another post that he most likely considered much more important and certainly more interesting. One day before taking the oath of office as the nation's vice president, Jefferson was installed as president of the American Philosophical Society (APS), a position he held for the next seventeen years. Headquartered in Philadelphia, at the time the temporary seat of the national government, the APS was thought by Jefferson to offer an escape from the tedium of the vice presidency (an "honorable and easy" position) and provide opportunity for him to engage in "philosophical evenings" with kindred souls.[53]

Among the concerns that attracted the attention of the APS was the matter of education in the new nation. A little more than a year before Jefferson's

Lithograph from J.C. Wild's View of Philadelphia: *"View from the State House (looking east over Philosophical Hall and Library Hall)," 1838. (Courtesy American Philosophical Society)*

election as its president, the society had arranged a contest with a prize of $100 to be awarded to the author of an essay best describing a system of education most ideally suited to the needs and character of the United States. On December 15, 1797, three days after returning from a trip to Monticello, Jefferson convened the meeting of the society at which the winner of the prize was to be announced. Two essays had been judged as being of "superior merit." Samuel Knox, a Presbyterian minister from Baltimore, shared the essay prize with Samuel H. Smith, soon to become the editor of the Jeffersonian *National Intelligencer.* Both essayists called for an extensive and uniform system of publicly supported schools reaching from the primary levels to academies and colleges and, at the apex of the system, a national university.[54]

The plans offered by Knox and Smith differed in detail, but the general schemes were similar and the project itself was not new. For several years Benjamin Rush, the learned Philadelphia physician and a signer of the Declaration of Independence, had been advocating a national system of schools and the creation of a national university. Four months before the delegates to the Constitutional Convention assembled in Philadelphia in 1787, Rush had published an article in *The American Museum.* Proclaiming that "THE REVOLUTION IS NOT OVER," Rush contended that a federal university was needed to disseminate knowledge of every kind throughout the country. The university should offer studies in history, the law of nature and nations, civil law, principles of commerce, and gunnery and fortifications. In this and later, more detailed proposals, Rush blended patriotism with calls for investigations into the sciences of agriculture, manufacturing, commerce, natural philosophy, and in the practical applications of chemistry. "We shall never restore public credit, regulate our militia, build a navy, or revive our commerce," he wrote, "until we remove the ignorance and prejudices, and change the habits of our citizens." This, he maintained, "can never be done until we inspire them with federal principles." Among the nearly five hundred subscribers to *The American Museum* were George Washington, Alexander Hamilton, Benjamin Franklin, James Madison, and Thomas Jefferson.[55]

The essays by Rush, Smith, Knox, and others put forth in the 1790s were echoing ideas that were very much in the air at the time. Particulars of various plans varied, but concern for bringing the people and states of the new union into closer harmony spurred a number of theorists to view publicly supported education—even the possibility of a national system of education—as being worthy of serious consideration. Essayists and political leaders eager to ensure that the citizens be educated in a systematic fashion directed most of their attention to government policy, but it was mostly via private and local initiatives that schools and colleges gradually spread across the nation. As Frederick Rudolph has emphasized, the leading educational theorists of the period conveyed "a deep sense of a nation being formed, a people's character being shaped." While they hoped that the general diffusion of knowledge would maximize happiness and assist able and deserving young men to attain positions of influence in society and government, they were in actuality much more concerned about the future of the nation than with the rise of individuals. These essayists, along with Jefferson, were searching for a system of education that would be suitable for coming generations of free and independent citizens intent on maintaining a republican society. They sought educational arrangements that would unite Americans as a people and as an expanding union of republics bound together by ties of interest, affection, and mutual consent. Jefferson, believing that the continuing existence and future prosperity of the new federal republic lay in the character of the people, was equally convinced that the people, to be virtuous and vigilant, needed to be educated in the principles and possibilities of republicanism.[56]

Chapter Five

EDUCATION FOR DEFENSE AND EXPANSION: WEST POINT AND THE NATIONAL UNIVERSITY IDEA

Science [knowledge] is more important in a republican than in any other government. And in an infant country like ours, we must much depend for improvement on the science of other countries, longer established, possessing better means, and more advanced than we are.

— THOMAS JEFFERSON TO [UNKNOWN
CORRESPONDENT], SEPTEMBER 28, 1821[57]

As the year 1800 dawned, Jefferson intensified his efforts to refine his thinking about and plans for the advancement of education. Jefferson at this time was encouraged by the fact that some of the "ablest and highest characters" in the state of Virginia had been contemplating the establishment of a public university. Sensing that the moment might be approaching when Virginia legislators might act favorably on such an undertaking, Jefferson sought to extend his understanding of the form and substance of a superior institution in which all the useful sciences could be taught at the very highest levels of knowledge. On January 18, 1800, he wrote to the illustrious scientist and Unitarian theologian, Dr. Joseph Priestley, with the announcement that "we wish to establish in the upper & healthier" and more central part of Virginia a university that would be based on a plan "so broad & liberal & *modern*, as to be worth patronizing with the public support, and be a temptation to the youth of other states to come and drink of the cup of knowledge & fraternize with us." Making clear to Priestley that he had abandoned all hope of reforming the College of William and Mary, Jefferson dismissed his alma mater as being "just well enough endowed to draw out the miserable existence to which a miserable constitution had doomed it." This new institution, Jefferson insisted, would be made of sterner stuff. Seeking Priestley's advice regarding the academic structure of the institution, Jefferson observed that "in an institution meant chiefly for use, some branches of science, formerly esteemed, may now be omitted; so may others now valued in Europe, but useless to us for ages to come."[58]

In his letter, Jefferson hastily listed courses, chiefly scientific, that struck him as being among the most useful and practical. His proposed list of studies included botany, chemistry, zoology, anatomy, surgery, medicine, natural philosophy, agriculture, mathematics, astronomy, geography, politics, commerce, history, ethics, law, arts, and fine arts. Jefferson implored Priestley to improve upon his initial listing of subject areas and to suggest the most efficient and economical arrangement of studies that would enable the university to bring the greatest amount of knowledge within the reach or "power of the fewest professors possible." Jefferson further observed that the initial faculty of this new university would consist of European scholars of "the first order of science" who would "follow no other calling" and thus would be expected to devote all of their time to academic instruction and research.

In another letter several days later, Jefferson noted that he did not mean to imply in his earlier listing that he thought the study of languages was without value. He explained that he thought the ability to read Latin and Greek authors in the original, while perhaps not essential to obtaining "eminent degrees of science," was nonetheless very useful toward it and in any event was a "luxury" in science "at least as justifiable as in architecture, painting, gardening, or the other arts." He reminded Priestley of his earlier plans for a comprehensive three-tiered system of education in Virginia and of his hope that, when each level was finally in operation, the "middle grade of education"—the secondary schools or district colleges—could attend to the teaching of "languages, geography, surveying, and other useful things of that grade; and then a single University for the sciences."[59]

Priestley's response, to which he gave the title "Hints Concerning Public Education," was rather general and may not have been particularly helpful, although Jefferson thanked Priestley by saying that his ideas "came up perfectly to what I had wished from you, and if they are not turned to useful account for posterity, it will be from the insensibility of others to the importance of good educa-tion." A point that may have impressed Jefferson was Priestley's recommendation that there be two classes of "public seminaries," one for specialized training in the professions and the other for gentlemen "who are designed for offices of civil and active life." The former institutions would be fewer in number but would require a larger number of more specialized professors, especially in the sciences, than would the liberal arts institutions. In acknowledging Priestley's recommendations, Jefferson assured him that "as soon as we can ripen the public disposition we shall bring forward our proposition."[60]

Within weeks of his request to Priestley, Jefferson delighted in a visit to Monticello by Pierre Samuel Du Pont de Nemours, an intimate associate from his days as minister to France. The old friends discussed Jefferson's aspirations for advancing education, a subject on which they focused much of their subsequent correspondence. In a letter written on April 12, 1800, Jefferson asked Du Pont to identify those branches of science "which in the present state of man, and particu-larly with us, should be introduced into an academy." He emphasized the neces-sity of arranging and "reducing the important sciences to as few professorships as possible, because of the narrowness of our resources." Du Pont need not consider subjects such as Greek, Latin, common arithmetic, music, fencing, and dancing, Jefferson said, for they could be learned in other settings. "I should also exclude those which are unimportant," he added, " and those which are acquired by reading alone, without the help of a master, such as ethics."[61]

Although Jefferson made it clear to Du Pont that he was not requesting a treatise on the subject of education, that is exactly what Du Pont composed. Du Pont criticized Europe's universities, asserting that they had become sterile "extinguishers of intelligence" with a reverence for "dead languages" and the "gib-berish" of metaphysics. Referencing Jefferson's own plans for Virginia, Du Pont emphasized the importance of publicly supported (as well as private) primary and secondary schools (academies or "colleges") throughout the states. Focusing on the national level, however, Du Pont advocated the creation of a national library, a botanical garden, and a museum that would contain chambers that could accom-modate meetings of a national philosophical society. Du Pont applied the term

"University" to the whole system, but specified that there should be four independent "special schools" for the higher sciences located in the nation's capital: schools of medicine, mines, social science and legislation, and one of "higher geometry [post Euclidian] and the sciences that it explains." This latter branch, the School of Transcendental Geometry, should provide a concentrated engineering curriculum with studies focused on transcendent geometry and the sciences dependent upon it such as astronomy, hydrology, navigation, construction and rigging of ships, and "engineering, both civil and military, for the artillery." The engineering professorships, Du Pont asserted, would form "the nucleus of an admirable Philosophic Society" that "will do wonderful things in a country where it will be so tremendously rewarded." Du Pont also observed that, in terms of engineering for military and civil construction, "no nation is in such need of canals as the United States" and most of the country's ports had "no means of exterior defense." Finally, Du Pont envisioned a "General Council of Education" composed of a representative from each state to serve as a coordinating body for this "University of North America." There would be two categories of students: those chosen for ability, who would receive scholarships funded by their states, and others who could attend at their own expense.[62]

Jefferson's interest in these and other educational plans was of necessity tempered by the realization that he had already been twice defeated in his efforts to get the Virginia legislature to enact his own comprehensive school plans. Although he tried to be optimistic, Jefferson had no way of knowing when, if ever, his state might push forward on plans for publicly supported elementary and secondary schools, much less act favorably on plans still in incubation regarding a state university. Up to this point, as his correspondence with Priestley and Du Pont in early 1800 reveals, Jefferson could only express the wish or hope—not anything approaching a developed plan—that *some* type of institution of advanced learning might be established *sometime* in the future *somewhere* in Virginia. A future that might (or might not) bring into existence the University of Virginia was uncertain and unknowable; the needs and possibilities of the present were more obvious.

As it happened, at the very time that Jefferson was soliciting advice from Priestley and Du Pont regarding the most advantageous arrangement of university studies that would crown the layered education system he had first envisioned in the 1770s, he was forced by circumstances to contemplate as well proposals from within the Adams administration regarding the founding of a military academy. The idea of establishing a military academy was by no means novel in 1800. Calls for a military academy dated back to the early days of the Revolutionary War, and the idea had been endorsed and encouraged repeatedly by George Washington. In 1776 John Adams had proposed that the Continental Congress form a committee to study a "plan for the Establishment of a military Academy, in the Army." Adams also wrote to Colonel Henry Knox that "I wish We had a military Academy, and should be obliged to you for a Plan of such an Institution. The expense would be a trifle, no object at all with me."[63]

Congressional inaction killed Adams's plan, but similar calls for a military academy echoed down through the years. Jefferson himself had given close (but unofficial) attention to a 1783 proposal submitted by General Frederick William von Steuben that called for the establishment of three military academies. Steuben had suggested that graduates of the proposed academies might apply for appointments in the regular Army, but recommended that the large majority should return to civilian life where they might "diffuse sound military opinion throughout the nation." Jefferson had been intrigued enough by this plan to make private calculations on the range of subject areas and the number and projected salaries of the instructional staff for these proposed institutions. He confided in his notes, however, that he thought it might be more reasonable to upgrade existing colleges to take care of these functions.[64]

When during the presidency of George Washington a proposal to establish a military academy was brought forward, Jefferson, as secretary of state, argued against the constitutionality of the measure. Twice in November 1793 Washington's cabinet discussed the idea. Although Washington was strongly inclined to push the project, Jefferson raised the constitutional question. Jefferson recorded that "the President said he would not choose to recommend anything against the Constitution," but if the constitutionality of the issue were merely "doubtful," Washington said that he would refer the matter to Congress and let that body decide "whether the Constitution authorized it or not."[65]

Although Congress did not heed Washington's pleas for a military academy, in the spring of 1795 it did enact a provision that provided for "books, instruments, and apparatus" and the extension of limited instruction to officer candidates stationed at West Point. In 1798, at the urging of Secretary of War James McHenry, Congress took another halting step toward military education by authorizing "four teachers of the arts and sciences necessary for the instruction of the artillerists and engineers." Determined to avoid appointing foreigners (especially Frenchmen) to the post, President Adams, after lengthy consideration, concluded that he could not find a single candidate who fully satisfied his expectations.[66]

Secretary of State Alexander Hamilton, meanwhile, had been at work developing his own plans for a "new and enlarged army" and the establishment of a military academy on a more elaborate and comprehensive scale than had yet been envisioned. He proposed creating an academy that would consist of five schools. A two-year School of Fundamentals would lay the foundation with instruction in mathematics and military arts. Upon completion of the basic course, cadets would be sent to one of the more advanced schools for additional training. Those in the School of Engineering and Artillery would continue for two more years in theoretical and field studies; those in the School of Cavalry or School of Infantry would complete one additional year concentrating on riding, fencing, and allied practical and tactical subjects. Cadets appointed to the School of the Navy would spend two additional years that combined advanced theoretical work with shipboard experiences. Hamilton forwarded his plan to Secretary McHenry in November of 1799. McHenry in turn sent the proposal to Congress along with an estimate of the funds he thought would be needed to put the plan into operation. Congress, however, adjourned in April 1800 without bringing the matter to the floor.[67]

Congressional delay did not deter Jefferson from giving renewed attention to the idea of a military academy. Although creating a military school certainly had not been of primary interest to Jefferson when he sought the advice of Priestley and Du Pont in the early months of 1800, it is equally certain that he was well informed about the details of Hamilton's plan, a proposal "almost the whole" of which he initially had dismissed as being "useless." Jefferson, however, could not fail to have had an interest in the arrangement or placement of sciences related to military arts and other fields of importance related to the security, development, and further expansion of the American empire for liberty. He shared with others a sense of embarrassment and uneasiness over the nation's deficiency of knowledge in engineering and other useful sciences. Attention to matters of military science and military preparedness was all the more a matter of concern in the climate of increasingly fragile relations on the western frontier as well as threats from abroad that marked the closing years of the eighteenth century.[68]

Although the lineage of the military academy project can be traced back at least to 1776, the most proximate proposal was of Hamiltonian design. Jefferson's assumption of the presidency in 1801 made it possible for him to scale back considerably Hamilton's proposal and thus convert a Federalist initiative into a mechanism that would serve Republican ends. As sponsor of the Military Peace Establishment Act of 1802, an act that, contrary to Hamilton's plan, reduced rather than expanded the size of the military, Jefferson laid the groundwork for an institution that would serve political and scientific as well as military ends. Not only would a military academy at West Point provide a route for the appointment of young Republicans into the officer ranks of the army, but with proper training in the sciences related to engineering, these officers could be prepared for leadership in advancing internal developments and national expansion as well as provide leadership for national defense. It is not without significance that Jefferson instructed his secretary, Captain Meriwether Lewis, to peruse the list of officers then in service and carefully note the political affiliation as well as the military qualifications of each. Those officers identified by Lewis as being among the most unfit in terms of military skill were dismissed from service. However, some who were militarily "qualified" but deemed to be fervent opponents of the new administration also lost their commissions. Jefferson was inclined to continue in service mainly those whose sympathies were conducive to advancing Republican rather than Federalist ideals.[69]

Jefferson's apparent reversal of stance regarding the appropriateness of establishing a military academy must be viewed not only in terms of political advantage but also in the context of his larger interest in educational progress. At the time of Jefferson's election and the "Revolution of 1800," he was steeped in educational ideas, plans, and proposals. As he wrote years later to his nephew, Peter Carr, with regard to renewed efforts that eventually culminated in the founding of the University of Virginia, Jefferson had "lost no occasion" of making himself

Colonel Jonathan Williams. *(Courtesy West Point Museum Art Museum, United States Military Academy)*

"acquainted with the organization of the best seminaries in other countries, and with the opinions of the most enlightened individuals" on both sides of the Atlantic. Thus, the educational plans of Priestley and Du Pont, and those of Rush, Smith, Knox, and others who advocated a national system of schools and a national university—as well as Jefferson's own continuously evolving designs for the advancement of science and enlightened republicanism in his native state—all take on new significance. Jefferson was absorbing—and refining—a variety of proposals and theories advanced by "wise and learned men." While none of the plans put forth by others could be adopted without change, the value of other proposals was their

service as examples from which selections might be made "which are good for us." In this way, Jefferson explained to his nephew, institutions could be arranged to correspond with our own social condition and then be improved and enlarged "in proportion to the encouragement [they] may merit and receive."[70]

Jefferson's designs for West Point can be discerned in large measure in his choice of Jonathan Williams as the founding superintendent of the academy. Williams, a moderate Federalist, had little military experience beyond having translated a French treatise on artillery and another on the elements of fortification. Appointed by Adams as a major in the Second Regiment of Artillerists and Engineers in February 1801, Williams had been in uniform less than three months when notified that Jefferson had selected him to serve as inspector of fortifications and officer in charge of the Corps of Engineers that was to constitute a military academy at West Point. He had, however, been known to Jefferson since their time together in Paris in the 1780s. The grandnephew of Benjamin Franklin, Williams had lived with and served as his uncle's research assistant while abroad. On their return voyage from Europe in 1785, Franklin and Williams had conducted experiments on the relationship between water temperature and ocean currents. Williams extended his research on later voyages and in 1799 published his findings as a book to aid in navigation. He also contributed essays to the *Transactions* of the American Philosophical Society and was serving as its secretary when Jefferson became the society's president. Correspondence between Williams and Jefferson touched on various scientific topics, including Jefferson's improved plow design and methods each had used to calculate the heights of mountains along the Blue Ridge of Virginia. After receiving from Williams a copy of his *Memoir on the Use of the Thermometer in Navigation* and his translation of Heinrich Otto Von Scheel's *Treatise of Artillery*, Jefferson acknowledged that he would "be very happy to see the corps of which he was a member profit by his example and pursue the line of information he [had] so well pointed out." By selecting Williams, Jefferson not only entrusted West Point to the care of a man with at least moderately acceptable political views, but he also made a practical-minded scientist the academy's first superintendent.[71]

Official provisions and expectations for the new military academy were modest at the outset. As initially established by the 1802 Military Peace Establishment Act, the United States Military Academy (USMA) was not created to train officers for all branches of the regular army or militia, or even the nucleus of a general officer corps. Instead, the USMA was to prepare a small number of cadets for duty in a narrow branch of technical service, the Corps of Engineers, which by law was limited initially to twenty members. The law left open the question of curriculum, directing only that "the necessary books, implements and apparatus for the use and benefit of the said institution" should be provided "at the public expense." That a great deal was left to the discretion of Major Williams is revealed in a letter he wrote to a fellow officer in which he confided that, other than instructions to use a specific mathematics text, "I have not received from the Secretary of War [Henry Dearborn], one word descriptive of the plan of the institution and the Education expected."[72]

Williams's hope that the USMA might become an important national scientific establishment clearly outdistanced the funds available for the project. Williams wanted the American ministers to England and France to seek the opinion of "the most eminent professional Men in London and Paris" regarding books and equipment and to purchase for the academy "every Book of merit that is extant, so far as is connected with the Profession." Although the administration determined that, financially, it could not authorize an undertaking as extensive as that envisioned by Williams, Jefferson personally reviewed Williams's initial request for books and implements, made comments in the margins that included additional recommendations, and returned the list to Williams with instructions for him to determine which items could be purchased in the United States and which could only be purchased in Europe. Secretary of War Dearborn repeatedly reminded Williams that, in light of "the present state of the Academy funds" appropriated by Congress, spending could not exceed what was absolutely necessary.[73]

In spite of the administration's stringent financial policies and the vagaries of the act of establishment, Williams, who was promoted to lieutenant colonel in July 1802, endeavored to do whatever he could to advance the academy as a scientific institution. His desire to transmit to the cadets a spirit of scientific inquiry and an awareness of the broad horizons their new profession offered was perhaps best exemplified by his establishment of the United States Military Philosophical Society (USMPS). "Our guiding star," Williams wrote, "is not a little mathemati-

Detail of View of West Point, *(1780) by Pierre Charles L'Enfant, Corps of Engineers officer. (Courtesy West Point Museum Art Collection, United States Military Academy)*

cal school, but a great national establishment …. We must always have it in view that our Officers are to be men of Science, and as such will by their acquirements be entitled to the notice of learned societies." On November 12, 1802, Williams presented the idea of forming a scientific society to the officers of the Corps of Engineers. The officers voted the society into existence and a week later elected Williams to the presidency.[74]

Within a month the USMPS adopted a constitution that made the officers and cadets of the Corps of Engineers members by right and the nucleus of the governing body. The constitution further provided that "any gentleman, provided he be a citizen of the United States, whether a military man or not," was eligible for membership. A few years later the society opened its ranks to non-U.S. citizens as well. The USMPS, patterned on the American Philosophical Society, was designed to supplement the educational and scientific activities of the Corps of Engineers. In time the society's library, the core of which consisted of Williams's private collection that contained some volumes he had inherited from Franklin, grew to hold the finest collection of technical works in the country.[75]

Williams immediately solicited President Jefferson's endorsement of the society. Explaining that its purpose was to preserve the elements of military science that veterans of the Revolution and travelers may have acquired, Williams invited Jefferson as president to become the "perpetual Patron" of the society. Jefferson's response was clearly supportive. Describing himself as "A friend of Science in all of its useful Branches, and believing that of the Engineer of great utility, I sincerely approve of the Institution of a Society for its Improvement," he wrote. He recognized that the society's membership would be small at the outset, but reasoned that as scientific inquiry was "directly in the line of their profession, and entitled to all their time," the officers and cadets would soon give ample evidence of the society's value. While stating that "it is not probable that I may be able to render it any service," he accepted "the Patronage you are pleased to propose" and again noted "the perfect coincidence" of the society's objects "with the legal duties" of its members. Jefferson concluded his note of acceptance by stating that sponsorship of the society was "consistent with the duties which I owe" to the USMA.[76]

All did not go smoothly for Williams, West Point, or the USMPS during the early years. Colonel Williams, incensed that his authority was limited to command over officers and cadets in the Corps of Engineers only and did not extend to all military personnel of lesser rank, at one point resigned his commission. The issue of command authority dated back to the Revolutionary War when all engineers in the employ of the American army were foreigners. Based on that circumstance, the tradition evolved whereby engineers were seen as staff officers without the authority to command troops. Although circumstances had changed by the time Williams had become the officer in charge of the Corps of Engineers and superintendent of the academy, the policy had not. Williams bristled when confronted with the fact that officers in other corps did not recognize his presumed authority. Following his resignation, Williams remained a private citizen for twenty-two months before accepting reappointment in the spring of 1805—even though the command issue had not been completely resolved and would cause him to resign once again in 1812. During the time of his absence, the academy went through a period of near ruin.[77]

Upon Williams's reinstatement on April 19, 1805, he immediately undertook to resurrect the USMPS and extend its influence and political standing by inviting into membership "the most distinguished characters in our country." While he initially considered making all members of Congress members of the society, he followed Jefferson's advice of making a "judicious selection of a few friends of science or lovers of the military art." Those so honored, Jefferson reasoned, would be inspired "with the desire of actively patronizing" the society's interests. Among the scores of well-known dignitaries extended membership in the USMPS that fall and in later months were both Federalists and Republicans, men who were known to have an interest in military preparedness, the advancement of science, and western exploration. Each member received an engraved certificate bearing the society's motto, "*Scientia in Bello Pax,*" translated by Williams as "Science in War is the Guarantee of Peace."[78]

Despite historians who later claimed that during Jefferson's administration West Point became the "center of scientific activity in America," the USMA might have been hard pressed to merit those accolades, and Williams and Jefferson believed that the institution was not being allowed to live up to its full potential.

Williams, complaining that the administration was not doing enough to strengthen the academy, campaigned repeatedly for its relocation to the nation's capital. It appears that both the academy's superintendent and Jefferson hoped that by enlisting so many legislators and men of scientific and military prominence as members of the USMPS, the inductees would use their influence to help relocate the academy to Washington. Williams and Jefferson wanted the USMA to become a national school of engineering along the lines earlier proposed by Du Pont and brought forward in 1806 by Joel Barlow (about whom more will be said below). A move to the nation's capital would place the academy directly under the protective eyes of Jefferson and Congress. Williams anticipated this possibility when he drew up the constitution for the USMPS with the proviso that its location would be "wherever the Military Academy shall be established."[79]

Through Secretary of War Dearborn, Jefferson endeavored to reassure Williams that moving the academy from West Point to Washington would occur in time. Williams, however, was often impatient with and unsure of Jefferson's commitment. However, he must have been encouraged when, in 1808, Jefferson asked Williams to submit a report on "the Progress and Present State of the Military Academy, with some suggested alternations." Williams complied with Jefferson's request and rehearsed the USMA's struggles to date. The superintendent noted that, if Congress had given the president power to appoint instructors and superintend the internal affairs of the academy, "we should, at this day, have a greater number of well instructed young officers than we can boast of." As it now stands, Williams lamented, the school is "like a foundling, barely existing among the mountains, and nurtured at a distance, out of sight, and almost unknown to its legitimate parents."[80]

Removal to Washington was not the only remedy suggested by Williams. He proposed that "the military academy be placed under the direction of the President of the United States in all that does or can relate to it, any thing contained in any former law to the contrary notwithstanding." He called for an expansion of the number of cadets to include civilians as well as military personnel, an increase in faculty positions, and an expansion of the curriculum to include additional work in French, German, chemistry, mineralogy, mathematics, nautical astronomy, geography, navigation, and engineering as part of a four-year curriculum. There could be no doubt about his intent of making the USMA into a great scientific institution.[81]

In transmitting Williams's report to Congress, Jefferson stated that "the idea suggested by him of removing the institution to this place" was worthy of attention. "Beside the advantage of placing it under the immediate eye of the government," Jefferson advised, a relocated academy would "render its benefits common to the naval department, and will furnish opportunities of selecting on better information, the characters most qualified to fulfill the duties which the public service may call for." While a bill to achieve these ends was before Congress, Jefferson assured Williams that "the state and interests in the Military Academy will not be forgotten." He proved to be true to his word. When Williams sent to Jefferson a transcription of an unsigned paper regarding militias in the belief that the document could be useful in swaying members of Congress to favor the removal and strengthening of the USMA, Jefferson informed him that, although he could not address the issue formally, he had taken the liberty of having "a sufficient number of copies printed to lay on the desk of every member without the least indication of the quarter from whence they came."[82]

Congress, however, was persuaded by neither Jefferson's overt nor covert efforts in behalf of Williams's plan. Many in Congress had no enthusiasm for establishing a national engineering school in Washington and certainly had reservations about giving to the president the extensive power that Williams had proposed. The bill died, and with it perished the dream of a national university with an affiliated military academy located in the nation's capital.

To appreciate more fully how Jefferson had come to embrace not only a military academy but to envision it as part of a national university scheme necessitates bringing into view the educational proposals of yet another of Jefferson's confidants, the poet and diplomat Joel Barlow. In 1800, at the same time that Jefferson was seeking the advice of Priestley and Du Pont, he had received correspondence from Barlow regarding the latter's dream of founding a great national institution in Washington. Ideas that were embryonic in 1800 did not take definite shape until several years later. By January 1806, however, four years after West

Point's founding, Barlow had developed his scheme into a *Prospectus of a National Institution to be Established in the United States*. Although Barlow's 1806 *Prospectus* was more elaborate than Du Pont's earlier plan, both shared the feature of having special schools, including a military academy, that would operate as components of a national university. In Barlow's plan, the military academy then in existence at West Point was to be moved to Washington. Barlow also called for a school of mines and a school of roads and bridges that would include studies in navigation, canals, and hydraulic architecture—a subject included at the suggestion of Robert Fulton, who, like Barlow, was a member of the USMPS. Barlow also proposed a conservatory of useful arts and trades, a museum of natural history, a museum of fine arts, a national library, a *prytaneum* (school of general science), a mint, an observatory, and district colleges scattered throughout the union that would be associated with the national institution in Washington. Barlow's plan also provided for the establishment of a printing press for the production and dissemination of scientific and scholarly researches as well as the publication of textbooks for use in elementary schools throughout the country. He maintained that cheap and widely distributed textbooks would "give a uniformity to the moral sentiment, a republican energy to the character, [and] a liberal cast to the mind and manners of the rising and following generations."[83]

Barlow met with Jefferson on February 23, 1806, to discuss the plan and get his endorsement. The next day Jefferson returned Barlow's bill for the establishment of a "National Academy & University at the City of Washington," along with "such alterations as we talked over last night." The alterations, Jefferson assured Barlow, were "chiefly verbal." The president encouraged Barlow by asserting that he had often wished to have a "Philosophical society or academy so organized as that while the central academy should be at the seat of government," associated institutions would be spread around the country. Publications from these more distinct academies could be presented to the central academy that could in turn disseminate the best to the other academies. "In this way," reasoned Jefferson, "all the members wheresoever dispersed might be brought into action, and an useful emulation might arise between the affiliated societies." Jefferson closed with the speculation that perhaps "the great societies now existing might incorporate themselves in this way with the National one." The prospect intrigued Jefferson, but he confessed that "time does not allow me to pursue this idea."[84]

Pennsylvania senator George Logan introduced a bill in March 1806 based on Barlow's *Prospectus,* but after three readings the bill died in committee. In his next annual message to Congress on December 2, however, Jefferson tried to revive the proposal by encouraging Congress to consider amending the Constitution if necessary in order to allow for federal expenditures in support of a national university and internal improvements. He urged Congress to think of public outlays for education and internal improvements as means whereby sectionalism could be reduced and union cemented "by new and indissoluble ties." He explained that "education is here placed among the articles of public care, not that it would be proposed to take its ordinary branches out of the hands of private enterprise, which manages so much better all the concerns to which it is equal," but rather because "a public institution can alone supply those sciences which, though rarely called for, are yet necessary to complete the circle, all the parts of which contribute to the improvement of the country, and some of them to its preservation."[85]

Once again Congress refused to follow Jefferson's lead. As one of Barlow's biographers would later put the matter, the failure of Congress to pursue the national university scheme proposed by Barlow and endorsed by Jefferson meant that the third president would have to "content himself" with setting up the University of Virginia during his retirement years. One need not agree that the University of Virginia was seen by Jefferson (or should be seen by us) as a mere consolation for the failure of larger and bolder educational visions, but it does seem evident that Jefferson had every reason to be discouraged with repeated rounds of legislative resistance at both the state and national levels. Yet he offered consolation to Barlow by noting, "there is a snail-paced gait for the advance of new ideas on the general mind, under which we must acquiesce." He observed that "a 40. year's experience of popular assemblies has taught me, that you must give them time for every step you take. If too hard pushed, they baulk, & the machine retrogrades." Jefferson's hope for governmental attention to education and other progressive developments in the future was tempered by his awareness that legislatures, if they acted at all, would probably show a preference for internal improvements: "People generally have more feeling for canals & roads," he mused, "than education."[86]

Although larger schemes considered by Jefferson and some of his associates did not materialize during his two terms as president, Jefferson departed from the White House with at least the hope that he had contributed in some degree to the diffusion of knowledge through his efforts that led to the founding of the United States Military Academy. He was honored years later by the academy when the faculty and cadets commissioned Thomas Sully to paint his portrait, which today appropriately hangs in the institution's library. Jefferson acknowledged the honor by remarking, "I have ever considered the establishment [USMA] as of major importance to our country and in whatever I could do for it, I viewed myself as performing a duty."[87]

Jefferson performed yet another educational duty while in the nation's service in Washington. Less glamorous and seldom acknowledged, Thomas Jefferson served as the founding president of the Washington, D.C. School Board. Elected by the City Council as a trustee and then president of the board when it was organized in August 1805, he personally contributed $200 toward the support of the first two schools that were initially constructed. In addition to soliciting contributions from public-minded citizens, the District of Columbia City Council placed a special tax on "slaves, dogs, licenses for carriages and hacks, for ordinaries and taverns, for retailing wines and spirituous liquors, for billiard tables, for theatrical and other amusements, and for hawkers and peddlers" to be used "for the education of the poor of the city." A report adopted by the board on September 19, 1805, indicated that the city's schools were envisioned to be part of a much larger system of education. The report declared that the board contemplated the establishment and endowment of "a permanent institution for the education of youth" in which "every species of knowledge essential to the liberal education of youth may, eventually, be acquired." Moreover, when completed, the institution would embrace "three great departments—Schools for teaching the rudiments of knowledge necessary to the common purposes of life; a College in which the higher branches may be taught; and a University, in which the highest and most splendid attainments may be acquired." The latter institution, it was hoped, might prove itself worthy of "national assistance."

It seems clear that in this report and in many subsequent actions that the board was well acquainted with and no doubt influenced by Jefferson's thinking on education, either directly or indirectly. His fingerprints were all over the proposal for a system of local public schools (public defined by the board as "a school supported wholly or in part at public expense") that would provide for the free education of poor students, a college that would teach a wide range of useful subjects, and a capstone university at the top of the pyramid that would be national in scope. Financial exigencies and local conditions occasioned shifting approaches and priorities, but the general scheme remained in view. Thus, even while performing the demanding duties of the nation's highest office, Thomas Jefferson continued to act on his belief that "knowledge promotes the happiness of man" and declared himself "to ever be exposed to contribute my endeavors towards its extension." [88]

Chapter Six

Retirement and Revival of Educational Plans for Virginia

There are two subjects indeed which I shall claim a right to further as long as I breathe, the public education and the subdivision of the counties into wards. I consider the continuance of republican government as absolutely hanging on these two hooks.

— Thomas Jefferson to Joseph C. Cabell, January 31, 1814[89]

If ever a man looked forward to retirement from public life, it was surely President Thomas Jefferson. As he was preparing to leave Washington at the end of his second term, he wrote to his old friend Du Pont: "Never did a prisoner, released from his chains, feel such relief as I shall on shaking off the shackles of power." Intending to leave behind the "boisterous ocean of political passions," Jefferson eagerly anticipated a life of retirement spent among his family, friends, books, and farms. "Nature intended me for the tranquil pursuits of science, by rendering them my supreme delight," Jefferson confided to Du Pont. Monticello, now mostly completed after four decades of "putting up and tearing down," was to be his sanctuary. Now, at last, he could live out the desire he had expressed even before entering the presidency: "all my wishes end where I hope my days will end, at Monticello."[90]

Jefferson's return to his family at Monticello—which then included his daughter Martha, her husband, and their eight children—and to his farms that consisted of approximately ten thousand acres of land worked by some two hundred slaves, was marked both by moments of tranquility and times of acute stress. Having turned the President's House into "a general tavern" for the Washington community during his presidency and prone to entertain and live beyond his means, Jefferson returned to Monticello carrying around $25,000 in unpaid obligations. With no pension, successive seasons of erratic weather that resulted in crop failures, provision of hospitality to a steady stream of visitors, and poor management of his personal finances, Jefferson was weighed down by the specter of insolvency as he approached the closing years of his life. The coup de grace came in 1818 when Jefferson, against his better judgment, endorsed notes for Wilson Cary Nicholas in the amount of $20,000. When Nicholas defaulted, Jefferson was left with this additional obligation. By the time of his death, he was more than $100,000 in debt.[91]

These burdens and the aches and inconveniences of age notwithstanding, Jefferson found time not only for the pleasures of family, friends, and books in his retirement years, but also for involvement in public projects. Chief among the items of unfinished business to which he began to redirect his attention was that of education. Soon after his retirement he wrote: "I have indeed two great measures at heart, without which no republic can maintain itself in strength." He listed as the first objective "that of general education, to enable every man to judge for himself what will secure or endanger his freedom." The second measure was fundamentally related to the first: "To divide every county into hundreds, of such size that all the children of each will be within reach of a central school in it." The hundreds, or wards, were to be "little republics," drawing every citizen into the conduct of local affairs so that, in truth, the people could govern themselves. Neither idea was new; both had been embedded in Jefferson's Bill for the More General Diffusion of Knowledge that he had first put forward back in 1779.[92]

Although of necessity Jefferson had been largely removed from the political affairs of his own locality and state during his presidential years, he had kept himself informed about—and given encouragement to—the efforts of associates who sought to advance the cause of education back home. Even during the years when he was overseeing the establishment of the United States Military Academy and giving consideration to the national university idea, he continued to check the pulse of his fellow Virginians regarding education-related measures there. An 1803 letter to a Geneva professor, Marc Auguste Pictet, reveals clearly that Jefferson's educational designs for Virginia, while thus far unrealized, had not been abandoned. "I have still had constantly in view to propose to the legislature of Virginia the establishment of one [good seminary of learning] on as large a scale as our present circumstances would require or bear," he wrote. Acknowledging that "as yet no favorable moment has occurred," Jefferson nonetheless asked the Genevan, as he had done previously of Priestley and Du Pont, for advice on a university curriculum.[93]

There were, of course, other leading Virginians who had pressed forward in Jefferson's absence on plans for the greater diffusion of knowledge among the people. In 1804, St. George Tucker, a noted jurist and George Wythe's successor to the professorship of law at William and Mary—and one who had long been dissatisfied with the location of the college, drafted a "Sketch of a Plan for the Endowment and Establishment of a State-University, In Virginia." Clearly influenced by Jefferson's earlier plans for Virginia, Tucker proposed locating a new university in a healthy part of the state "not more than 25 miles eastward of the blue ridge mountains ...."[94]

Tucker was in league with politician (and future governor) Littleton W. Tazewell, among others, regarding plans to push for a "grand seminary" in Virginia. In a Christmas Eve letter in 1804, Tazewell confided to Jefferson that considerable profit from the state's interest in Virginia canal companies, dividends generated by state-owned shares of the Bank of Virginia, escheats, and other potential sources of revenue had perhaps softened legislative resistance to educational projects. Tazewell suggested that the time might be ripe for friends of education to establish a "great seminary of learning, and such subordinate institutions as may be deemed necessary." Tazewell further confided to Jefferson that, while the exact site for the university had not been determined, it would likely be "somewhere within a square of twenty miles" below the Blue Ridge with the town of Charlottesville being its easternmost border. Tazewell concluded his letter by counseling Jefferson to hold in confidence the intelligence he had transmitted. The need for confidentiality was needed, Tazewell said, "because it is sometimes necessary to conceal the healing medicine from the patient, lest his sickly appetite may reject that which alone may bring him health and life." Jefferson understood all too well the political truth underlying Tazewell's medical metaphor and used it himself when describing his own attempts to prescribe curative educational measures for the benefit of his fellow citizens.[95]

Although still determined to remain behind the scenes, Jefferson responded immediately to Tazewell's letter by proclaiming that no one could be "more rejoiced" than he at the information that the legislature of Virginia might be ready to initiate a university "on a liberal plan." Echoing a familiar refrain, Jefferson wrote: "Convinced that the people are the only safe depositories of their own liberty, & that they are not safe unless enlightened to a certain degree, I have looked on our present state of liberty as a short-lived possession unless the mass of the people could be informed to a certain degree." Stressing again the need for local schools to enable every member of society "to read, to judge & to vote understandingly" on current issues, Jefferson acknowledged that the plan outlined by Tazewell considered only the level of university education. Given conditions of the moment and setting forth a pragmatic strategy, Jefferson concurred: "Let us receive with contentment what the legislature is now ready to give. The other branch will be incorporated into the system at some more favorable moment."[96]

As requested by Tazewell, Jefferson offered advice regarding curriculum, governance, financing, and other aspects of the contemplated university. Emphasizing that the subjects should be selected with an eye toward utility, he observed that "What was useful two centuries ago is now become useless, e.g., one half the professorships of Wm. & Mary. What is now deemed useful will in some of its parts become useless in another century." While recommending that most details of the institution should be left in the hands of a small number of trustees, he informed Tazewell that he had been collecting advice from Priestley, Du Pont, and other correspondents from Edinburgh, Geneva, and France. Jefferson expressed a preference for European professors and even offered comments regarding the design of the institution. Rejecting the common pattern of erecting a large building to house the university, Jefferson proposed basing the institution on a village concept. "A plain small house for the school & lodging of each professor is best," he advised.

"These connected by covered ways out of which the rooms of the students should open would be best," he noted, adding that in this fashion additional rooms could be built as needed. Jefferson's enthusiasm for the project was underscored by his notice to Tazewell that "I shall have a valuable legacy to leave it [the university], to wit, my library, which certainly has not cost less than 15,000 dollars."[97]

Jefferson's enthusiasm and generosity were not yet to be met in kind by the Virginia legislature, however. While other Virginia notables, including governors James Monroe (1799-1802) and William H. Cabell (1805-1808), also issued calls for attention to the "need of literary institutions" in the state during the years of Jefferson's presidency, no appreciable progress was made until the year following his retirement. In the fall of 1809, Jefferson visited with Governor John Tyler, who had long been a supporter of his educational agenda. In December Tyler urged the legislature to take action on behalf of public education. He berated the legislature for "its failure, by reason of a fatal apathy and a parsimonious policy, to provide state schools" and declared that "a stranger might think we had declared war against the Arts and Sciences." A bill that had been reported out of committee that fall authorizing the appropriation of "certain escheats, penalties, and forfeitures [to be directed] to the encouragement of learning" gained approval in the House of Delegates on January 29, 1810, and was passed by the Senate on February 8. Authorship of this act, which created "The Literary Fund of Virginia," has been variously attributed to House Speaker James M. Barbour, a progressive champion of schools for the general population, and Charles Fenton Mercer, also a proponent of popular education and a staunch Federalist. While both men claimed credit for this particular bill, Jefferson's influence and Tyler's pointed message no doubt played important roles in shaping the outcome.[98]

However credit for the creation of the Literary Fund might be apportioned, it is not without significance that a member of the legislative committee that reported the Literary Fund bill to the floor of the House was a young delegate representing Albemarle County, Joseph C. Cabell. A brother to Governor William H. Cabell, Joseph was a close friend of Isaac Coles, Jefferson's secretary and chief of staff during his second administration. Ties between the Cabells and Jeffersons dated back to the days when Peter Jefferson and Joseph's grandfather, William, were local surveyors, pioneering landowners, and justices of the peace. Joseph Cabell, who professed to Coles in 1807 that "the favorite object of my life is the amelioration of Education, and the diffusion of knowledge among the people," became not only Jefferson's ally but in time carried the burden of being his chief

legislative spokesman as they joined forces to realize, at least in part, what became their shared vision during Jefferson's final years. The collaboration between Jefferson and Cabell eventually led to the founding of the University of Virginia, but the course that had to be taken to reach that point was far from straight and smooth as will be explained in greater detail in the following chapters.[99]

Even so, the establishment of the Literary Fund in 1810 laid the foundation for all future state school legislation. Although an act adopted the next year registered a "solemn protest" against any attempt to use the Fund for any other purpose than that of the *Education of the*

Joseph C. Cabell. *(Courtesy Special Collections, University of Virginia)*

Poor," the act also proved to be a step forward toward the eventual establishment of the University of Virginia. For the first few years, however, even with additional funds derived from a state lottery, the Fund was too meager to be of any service. The War of 1812 diverted both interest and resources of the state away from educational concerns. Governor James Barbour, falling in line with a lengthening list of chief executives, took the legislature to task once again in an 1812 message by noting that still "no effort has been made to foster the means of education ...." Not until 1816, when buoyed by a swell in available funding made possible by the federal government, were Jefferson, Cabell, and other supporters of publicly funded education able to steer a more promising course that led to the founding of the University of Virginia.[100]

Before those momentous events occurred, however, Jefferson had struck out in yet another direction that also held promise of pointing the way toward

View from Monticello Looking Toward Charlottesville *(1825) by Jane Braddick Peticolas. (Thomas Jefferson Foundation)*

the eventual founding of his university in Charlottesville. A letter written to Dr. Thomas Cooper on January 16, 1814, strongly hinted at Jefferson's priorities as the new year began. Cooper, a Unitarian, had migrated to Pennsylvania from England in 1794 with his father-in-law, Joseph Priestley, to escape religious and political persecution. Admiring Cooper for his scientific, legal, and philosophical sophistication—as well as for his political and religious ideas—Jefferson had drawn him into his circle of regular correspondents. In his January 16 letter, Jefferson, using language similar to that employed in his letters to his English and French advisors fourteen years earlier, informed Cooper that "I have long had under contemplation, and been collecting materials for the plan of a university in Virginia which should comprehend all the sciences useful to us, and none others." Although he noted that there was talk of introducing such a measure in the current session of the legislature, he expressed his doubts that this might occur right away. However, should it happen, he wrote to Cooper, "it would offer places worthy of you, and of which you are worthy." Moreover, he intimated that the institution might possibly be able to purchase the scientific apparatus and books in Priestley's library. Jefferson stated that he would certainly make his own collection of seven or eight thousand volumes, "the best chosen collection of its size probably in America," available to the institution. Perhaps most significantly in terms of developments that occurred later in the spring and summer, Jefferson again noted the requirement of a healthy and central location and suggested that "the neighborhood of this place [Charlottesville]" would be ideal. Later in January, in two separate letters, Jefferson expressed to Cabell his belief that public education and the subdivision of counties into wards were essential to the continuance of republican government. In August Jefferson again wrote to Cooper, this time more optimistically stating that "We are about to make an effort for the introduction of [an] institution" in which "all the branches of science useful *to* us, and *at this day*, should be taught in their highest degree." As he had done with other members of his enlightened circle, Jefferson then asked Cooper to contribute his views on which subjects he thought to be of most worth.[101]

That these letters contained old themes is unquestionable. But what was new in the equation by 1814 was Jefferson's decision to become more directly and personally involved with an educational enterprise at the local level and, through that activity, to influence the direction of statewide developments. In the spring of 1814, Thomas Jefferson accepted an invitation to join the board of trustees of Albemarle Academy. The move to become a patron of this local secondary school placed Jefferson in a position that enabled him to set the course for what became the University of Virginia. While his epistolary missives and behind-the-scenes efforts to upgrade education in Virginia by no means abated, his more direct maneuverings that oriented the future direction of Albemarle Academy provided Jefferson with yet another point of entry through which he could advance his educational project. Jefferson, whose long years of advocacy of plans for the more general diffusion of knowledge had clearly earned him recognition as an educational statesman, now put his hands to the helm as an educational politician. He personally undertook to pilot Albemarle Academy out of the relatively safe harbor of local institutional waters into the much more uncertain and turbulent seas of state politics. The destination was unclear to all but Jefferson, who had set his bearing on a course leading to the University of Virginia.

Chapter Seven

Toward the Establishment of the University of Virginia: From Albemarle Academy to Central College

When sobered by experience I hope our successors will turn their attention to the advantages of education. I mean education on the broad scale, and not that of the petty academies, as they call themselves, which are starting up in every neighborhood .... I hope the necessity will at length be seen, here as in Europe, where every branch of science, useful at this day, may be taught in its highest degrees.

— Thomas Jefferson to John Adams, July 5, 1814[102]

The Old Stone Tavern across from the court house in Charlottesville was a popular eating and drinking establishment for local residents of Albemarle County. There was nothing unusual in the fact that on March 25, 1814, five prominent citizens of the community gathered there to discuss strategies for resurrecting a private academy that had been chartered by the Virginia legislature in 1803. Albemarle Academy had been given a name, but the school was stillborn. For eleven years it had existed on paper only. The original members of the board of trustees had been reduced to the five who on that March afternoon gathered at the tavern to discuss the possibility of actually giving life to the institution. There is no evidence to suggest that, prior to that afternoon, Thomas Jefferson had been involved in any way with plans for the academy.

The conventional explanation as to how Jefferson happened to become engaged in the fortunes of Albemarle Academy is, however, as questionable as it is plausible. According to historian Philip A. Bruce and others who have followed his lead, Jefferson just happened to stop off at the tavern while out on a customary afternoon horseback ride. As Bruce relates it, Jefferson's participation in the meeting of the trustees was "wholly accidental and unexpected." One of the trustees was said to have seen Jefferson riding by and, aware of his interest in education, asked him to dismount and join in the discussion then going on inside. Jefferson did so, allowed his name to be put forward with others to fill vacancies on the board, and at a subsequent meeting on April 5 was confirmed as a trustee and appointed to head a committee to draft rules and regulations and propose fundraising strategies for the institution.[103]

Perhaps it happened just that way. But it seems reasonable to suggest that Jefferson, whose nephew Peter Carr was among the five at the meeting and was elected by them as chairman of the Albemarle Academy board, was quite likely

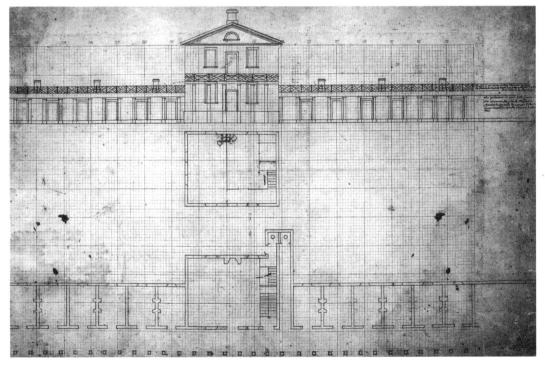

"Elevation and Plan Showing Typical Pavilion and Dormitories" (1814) by Thomas Jefferson, approved by the trustees of Albemarle Academy on August 19, 1814. (Courtesy Jefferson Papers, Special Collections, University of Virginia)

well aware of the time and place of the meeting. It is probably closer to the truth to suggest that Jefferson "invited himself" to the meeting, however casual and coincidental the occurrence may have been staged to appear. As his correspondence with Cooper and Cabell in the preceding months indicated, Jefferson clearly had been looking for an opening that would enable him to push his educational ideas forward. Membership on the Albemarle Academy board afforded him just such an opportunity.[104]

Although the academy board met several times over the next few months following its first full meeting on April 5, Jefferson did not attend again until August 19. By that time, Jefferson was prepared to come forward with an architectural drawing for the proposed academy—even though he was not a member of the committee charged with selecting the location. While the site selection committee had been vacillating between recommending that the Old Stone Tavern be purchased for use as the school (most likely their original intent) versus building a new structure located further away from the town, the board's acceptance of Jefferson's design on August 19 effectively sabotaged the former scheme. Jefferson's architectural drawing was almost identical to the one he had verbalized nearly ten years earlier in his letter of January 5, 1805, to Littleton Tazewell. Moreover, in 1810 Jefferson had offered this same basic plan in more detail when the trustees of a college in east Tennessee contacted him regarding distributing lottery tickets in support of the institution they were inaugurating. In the letter to Judge Hugh White of the Tennessee college's trustees, Jefferson volunteered unsolicited advice:

> I consider the common plan followed in this country, but not in others, of making one large and expensive building, as unfortunately erroneous. It is infinitely better to erect a small and separate lodge for each separate professorship, with only a hall below for his class, and two chambers above for himself; joining these lodges by barracks for a certain portion of the students, opening into a covered way to give a dry communication between all the schools. The whole of these arranged around an open square of grass and trees, would make it, what it should be in fact, an academical village, instead of a large and

common den of noise, of filth and of fetid air. It would afford that quiet retirement so friendly to study, and lessen the dangers of fire, infection and tumult. Every professor would be the police officer of the students adjacent to his own lodge, which should include those of his own class of preference, and might be at the head of their table, if, as I suppose, it can be reconciled with the necessary economy to dine them in smaller and separate parties, rather than in a large and common mess. These separate buildings, too, might be erected successively and occasionally, as the number of professorships and students would be increased, or the funds become competent.

Although the trustees of the college that later became the University of Tennessee were not impressed with Jefferson's novel design for their institution, the Albemarle Academy trustees adopted Jefferson's plan for an "academical village" as the arrangement "best suited to the purpose, provided the work can be completed according to the terms of the estimate."[105]

However slowly it may have dawned on the Albemarle Academy trustees that Jefferson's designs both on paper and in his head were for something much more impressive than just another "petty academy," several of Jefferson's correspondents were better informed. On July 5 Jefferson had written to his old friend John Adams complaining of institutions that sent students out into society with just enough learning "to be alienated from industrious pursuits, and not enough to do service in the ranks of science." Jefferson pointedly directed a barb toward academy teachers who, with some knowledge of Latin and perhaps a little of Greek, geography, and basic mathematics, "imagine and communicate this as the sum of science." It was only six days after the board meeting at which Jefferson had laid out his architectural designs for the academy that he wrote to Cooper informing him that an effort was underway to launch a university in which "all the branches of sciences useful to *us*, and *at this day*" would be taught at the highest possible level. Although it is unlikely that the Albemarle trustees (with the possible exception of Peter Carr) were yet aware of Jefferson's plans for their academy, the Sage of Monticello clearly was focusing on elevating their sights and transforming their institution into an establishment far different from what they had been discussing at the Old Stone Tavern back in the early spring.[106]

In a letter dated September 7, 1814, two weeks after informing Cooper that he was on the verge of establishing a university, Jefferson unveiled his larger project to the academy's board through a letter to its chairman, Peter Carr. Stating again the theme he had now rehearsed so often with some of his most knowledgeable confidants, Jefferson reiterated to his nephew his hope that their native state "would take up the subject of education" in such a fashion that "every branch of science, deemed useful at this day, should be taught in its highest degree." He reminded his associates of his 1779 proposal that called for the establishment of publicly funded elementary schools in every locality; of the ineffectiveness of the 1796 bill eventually adopted by the legislature; of his conviction that it was the duty of the state to provide every citizen with an education "proportioned to the condition and pursuits of his life;" and expressed the hope that such a comprehensive plan might again be brought forward someday "in a more promising form."[107]

The immediate object of the Albemarle Academy board, Jefferson reasoned, should be to determine just how their institution, in view of future ambitions and prospects as well as present circumstances and constraints, might best fit into a comprehensive statewide arrangement of schools encompassing elementary, general (secondary and collegiate), and advanced or professional studies. It seemed obvious to Jefferson, and he assumed to the academy trustees, that "with the first grade of education [elementary] we shall have nothing to do." Those members of society he labeled the "laboring classes" would, at the conclusion of their publicly supported period of elementary education, enter into agricultural pursuits, skilled apprenticeships, or other occupations. Members of the "learned classes" would continue with more advanced studies at the secondary or collegiate level. It was to these students and the "sciences of the second grade" that Jefferson suggested Albemarle Academy direct its efforts.[108]

In far greater detail than he had done in his 1779 bill, Jefferson advised Carr, and through him, the board, of the objectives and arrangement of courses that ought to be the focus in the second and third levels of his hierarchical scheme. Perhaps reflecting the influence of John Locke, Jefferson observed that the learned class could itself be subdivided into two sections: "those who are destined for the learned professions" and "the wealthy, who, possessing independent fortunes, may aspire to sharing in conducting the affairs of the nation, or to live with usefulness and respect in the private ranks of life." Jefferson advised that both of these groups needed instruction in "all the higher branches of science" and that all should therefore be taught in the general schools at least "to a competent degree."[109]

At the close of the general (or what Jefferson was now referring to as the collegiate) level of education, the wealthy would retire "with a sufficient stock of knowledge to improve themselves to any degree to which their views may lead them," Jefferson advised. Those destined to enter professional callings would continue on with their education "with more minuteness and detail than was within the scope of the general schools." "In these professional schools," Jefferson counseled, "each science is to be taught in the highest degree it has yet attained." Here would be prepared the lawyers, theologians, physicians, military leaders, agricultural scientists, architects, musicians, artists, and others who required advanced study in particular fields of endeavor.

In introducing the term "college" into his description of the second level of education, Jefferson was doing more than merely substituting a term sometimes used interchangeably with the words "academy" and "seminary" in the loose nomenclature of the day. Jefferson was planting the idea that the Albemarle Academy should contain the seeds of a collegiate-level institution, and within that, the germ of an even higher level university. He noted that the studies to be offered in the academy would at the outset have to reflect the "slender beginnings" of the institution and would need to be grouped in such a fashion as would enable each "professor" to instruct in as many of the related areas of study within his discipline as might be feasible. Jefferson suggested that as the institution matured and its financial means increased, however, the subjects should be subdivided until such point that "each professor shall have no more under his care than he can attend to with advantage to his pupils and ease to himself." In other words, both the corps of professors and range of studies would, over time, of necessity increase and each professor would be enabled to specialize ever more deeply into his particular domain of knowledge. Jefferson's refashioned academy would thus embody at the

Detail from Thomas Jefferson's letter to Peter Carr, September 7, 1814. (Courtesy Library of Congress)

outset an orientation toward collegiate status and in due course would evolve into a university embracing every science and branch of useful knowledge, each taught by an expert in a specialized discipline or professional area of study.

In setting forth the domain of the initial faculty, Jefferson recommended four areas of study each under a separate professor, viz:

I. Professorship

> *Languages and History, ancient and modern.*
>
> *Belles-Lettres, Rhetoric and Oratory.*

II. Professorship

> *Mathematics pure* (to include algebra, geometry, and trigonometry), *Physico-Mathematics* (to include mechanics, statics, hydrostatics, hydrodynamics, navigation, astronomy, geography, optics, pneumatics, acoustics), *Physics, Anatomy, Medicine, Theory.*

III. Professorship

> *Chemistry, Zoology, Botany, Mineralogy.*

IV. Professorship

Philosophy (to include ideology, ethics, law of nature and nations, government, and political economy).

Beyond these general studies, Jefferson stated, all students should engage in physical exercise and should be given instruction in military tactics "under a standing organization as a military corps" staffed by proper officers. While West Point might provide the nation with an officer corps of highly trained military engineers, Jefferson thought all non-military colleges should still provide training for civilians who would serve for limited periods of time as officers in the state militias and regular army.[110]

It is worth nothing that, in addition to these college-level courses designed for members of the "learned class," Jefferson also proposed that "a school for the deaf, dumb, and blind" should be connected to the professorship in languages. Moreover, he envisioned a school of technical philosophy that would offer specialized lectures in the evening to artisans who needed instruction that was more practical and less theoretical than that offered at the professional or university level. He recommended that this school, maintained wholly at public expense on the same basis as the ward schools, should offer lectures in the evening "so as not to interrupt the labors of the day." To this school would come "the mariner, carpenter, shipwright, pumpmaker, clockmaker, machinist, optician, metallurgist, founder, cutler, druggist, brewer, vintner, distiller, dyer, painter, bleacher, soapmaker," and a host of other artisans who wanted to learn more of the sciences that informed their occupational callings. Even while eyeing in the long term a university that would offer instruction at the very highest levels, Jefferson was cognizant of the practical benefits and applied uses of knowledge for the mass of the population. Until a complete system of education could be effected, Albemarle Academy would reach outward as well as upward.

Just as his 1814 academy proposal differed in some particulars from his 1779 bill, future renditions of Jefferson's proposed curriculum would vary in detail regarding the exact arrangement and scope of studies. Changing political strategies and fiscal circumstances as well as Jefferson's own more sharply defined sense of academic priorities explain shifts from one version to the next in later compilations of his proposals. His inclusion of theology in his 1814 curriculum proposal, for example, was dropped in later renderings in accordance with his own more honest views on the subject as well as upon the recommendation of his Unitarian friend and advisor, Thomas Cooper. Jefferson defended his initial inclusion of theology in his Carr letter by explaining to Cooper "[W]e cannot always do what is absolutely best. Those with whom we act, entertaining different views, have the power and the right of carrying them into practice. Truth advances, and error recedes step by step only; and to do to our fellow men the most good in our power we must lead where we can, follow where we cannot and still go with them, watching always the favorable moment for helping them to another step." Similarly, while he did not abandon the concept, concerns for economy and simplicity of curriculum prompted him to drop the call for a school of technical philosophy from later plans. The curriculum for the academy, college, and university envisioned by Jefferson was an evolving one. Thus, attentive as he was to curriculum, Jefferson's primary and most immediate intention in his letter to Carr was not to establish a fixed curriculum but rather to convince the trustees of the wisdom of expanding their vision and petitioning the legislature for a new charter that would convert their academy into a college in both name and aspiration. His letter to Peter Carr, termed by historian Herbert B. Adams as "the most important document in the early history of the University of Virginia," achieved that purpose.[111]

Following board acceptance of Jefferson's plan, Chairman Carr forwarded documents advancing Jefferson's plans to David C. Watson, a friend and legislator from neighboring Louisa County, for presentation to the legislature. Among these papers were petitions prepared by a board committee composed of Jefferson, his son-in-law Thomas Mann Randolph, and nephew Peter Carr seeking approval to receive proceeds from the sale of specified glebe lands, interest on monies that went into the Literary Fund from forfeitures, escheats, and defaults collected in Albemarle County, and the use of lottery proceeds as funding sources for the revamped institution—in addition to subscriptions or donations authorized by the initial chartering act of 1803. The proposed lottery scheme was more than a little devious. One hundred forty-seven local citizens had signed a petition in support of the lottery, thinking the proceeds would benefit the genial owner of the Old Stone Tavern, Triplett Estes, whose desire to sell the building to the academy trustees for use as a school was apparently a well known fact. Jefferson did nothing to abuse the Albemarle citizenry of that notion even though the board had by then effectively rejected the tavern site in favor of a yet unknown location that would accommodate Jefferson's "academical village" concept.[112]

In preparing the draft bill for legislative consideration, Jefferson included a statement calling for a reduction in the size of the board of trustees. As he had indicated in his Revisal Bill 80 regarding the reform of William and Mary thirty-five years earlier, Jefferson wanted a small governing board appointed by the legislature that would be "public" in terms of its outlook and responsibilities. Obviously this measure was designed to prefigure the institution's change of status from that of just another provincial academy to eventual standing as a state-sponsored institution of significance.

Perhaps the most telling item in the proposed legislation was the request that the name of the institution be changed from Albemarle Academy to Central College. Not only did the term "college" resound with a more elevated tone than "academy," but the choice of the term "central" conveyed the sense that this institution was more conveniently located than the three other colleges then existing in state: William and Mary in Williamsburg, Washington College in Lexington, and Hampden-Sydney College located sixty miles southwest of Richmond. While some on the board sought to honor Jefferson by adopting the title "Jefferson College," the architect of the plan emphatically insisted that "Central" should be the appropriate title. Jefferson's opinion prevailed.[113]

Severe illness incapacitated Peter Carr during the fall of 1814, and in February 1815, the academy's chairman died. Delegate Watson, to whom he had entrusted the critical papers pertaining to the conversion of the academy into a college, had for unknown reasons held back on presenting a bill to the legislature. On January 5, 1815, Jefferson, wondering why the documents had not been presented to the legislature, wrote to his young protégé and now senator representing Albemarle County, Joseph Cabell, and included copies of the papers earlier given to Watson. The package included a copy of Jefferson's September 14 letter to Carr, a communication he had received from Cooper in response to Jefferson's solicitation of his advice regarding curriculum matters, a copy of the trustee's petition to the legislature, and a copy of the draft legislation that embodied the changes being sought.

Jefferson, now turning to Cabell "as the main pillar" of support for the project, informed the young legislator that he already held the power to attract "three of the ablest characters in the world to fill the higher professorships" in the college. Jefferson had indeed been in correspondence with Jean-Baptiste Say regarding the possibility of the French economist relocating to Charlottesville. He knew as well that Thomas Cooper might seriously consider an offer to join the faculty of this new institution. Possibly the third "character" that Jefferson had in mind was Count Destutt de Tracy, with whose writings he was greatly impressed. Excited about the possibilities, Jefferson wrote to Cabell that, "With these characters, I should not be afraid to say that the circle of sciences composing that second, or general grade, would be more profoundly taught here than in any institution in the United States, and I might go further."[114]

Cabell answered Jefferson's letter on March 5 and noted that he had heretofore heard almost nothing of Jefferson's plan, but if he had been given responsibility of guiding the bill through the legislature, he would have given the matter "the greatest attention imaginable, and done anything in the compass of my feeble abilities to promote your views." Cabell counseled further that he could foresee no serious objections to the Central College bill, although some might challenge the request that the proceeds from the sale of glebe lands be used to establish the institution at Charlottesville, or have reservations about using Literary Fund monies for a project not directly related to the education of the poor. Some might also object to the loan of seven or eight thousand dollars that Jefferson suggested might be needed to attract the "ablest characters" for the professorships. As a graduate of the College of William and Mary, Cabell confessed that he hoped his alma mater would not be negatively affected by the new institution other than through the natural competition that would result from the existence of another college in the state. In a letter some months later to his old friend and classmate Isaac Coles, Cabell indicated that he had overcome whatever conflict of loyalties he may have felt initially and that "I shall do everything in my power to give success to Mr. Jefferson's scheme of a college now pending before the Assembly. The more the better. He has drafted a beautiful scheme of a college in Charlottesville."[115]

Cabell underestimated the opposition that Jefferson's plans would face in the legislature. The Central College bill was introduced into the House of Delegates in December 1815 by Thomas W. Maury of Albemarle and under the watchful eye of Senator Cabell. The House committee to which the bill was referred had no difficulty with the charter and name change, but did not sanction an appropriation from the Literary Fund. Cabell advised Maury "not to press that subject." With the appropriation measure deleted, the House quietly approved the bill.[116]

Before the bill was referred to the Senate, Cabell was approached by the other Albemarle delegate, Col. Charles Yancey, who expressed a different concern. Jefferson, unhappy with the ineffective 1796 law that had left it up to county court officials to determine if and when to launch elementary schools, had proposed that Central College be empowered to initiate and oversee public elementary education in Albemarle County. His bill for the reform of William and Mary had contained a similar oversight measure. In both instances the idea was not only to enable the top institution to coordinate and monitor the lower schools, but to remove from the wealthy members of the counties the power to block funding for elementary schools out of the belief that publicly funded schools were "a plan to educate the poor at the expense of the rich." Jefferson later explained to Cabell that he hoped also that the establishment of elementary schools in Albemarle would set an example and lead to the creation of elementary schools all across the state. Yancey, however, objected to having his county singled out from all other Virginia counties in this respect and convinced Cabell to strike the measure. In a similar fashion, Cabell also withdrew a Jeffersonian provision that would have allowed the proctor of Central College to serve as a justice of the peace with the power to imprison students. This latter feature was borrowed from European university custom and was designed both to keep order in the college precincts and, as Jefferson explained to Cabell, "to shield the young and unguarded student from the disgrace of the common prison, except where the case was an aggravated one." Hoping to smooth the way as much as possible for the passage of the more vital elements in the

Central College bill, Cabell pulled these controversial provisions rather than risk defeat at the hands of his Senate colleagues.[117]

Although altered from its original form in several respects, the bill creating Central College became law on February 14, 1816. Literary Fund support, trustee control of elementary schools in Albemarle County, and bestowal of justice of the peace powers on the college proctor were among casualties of legislative compromise. Jefferson himself recommended abandoning the proposal of a school for the deaf, dumb, and blind when that measure became entwined with a proposal to purchase the Old Stone Tavern for use by that school as an appendage to the college. Although he had proposed such a school in his letter to Peter Carr, Jefferson now reasoned that the "objects of the two institutions [the college vs. the special school] are fundamentally distinct. The one is science; the other, mere charity. It would be gratuitously taking a boat in tow, which may impede, but cannot aid the motion of the principal institution." [118]

Modified in these particulars, the bill sanctioned by the legislature did result in the conversion of Albemarle Academy, a secondary school that had no faculty, students, books, buildings or funds, into Central College. The trustees, or visitors as they were termed in the authorization law, were to be appointed by the governor, serve three-year terms, and be limited to six members, two-thirds fewer in number than had been authorized for the Albemarle Academy board. The visitors were granted power to appoint officers of the college, establish professorships, determine salaries and fees, establish a curriculum, and in general "to direct and do all matters and things which to them shall seem best for promoting the purposes of the institution ...."[119]

A long-time Jefferson ally and governor of the state, Wilson Cary Nicholas, had the responsibility of appointing the initial board of visitors of Central College. Jefferson, not wanting to alienate the former members of the academy's board of trustees but yet eager to have as co-visitors a small group of men of large reputation who would side with him in the contests ahead, worked through the board's secretary, Frank Carr, to place before the governor a select list of candidates. A month after Central College received legislative approval, Carr informed Nicholas that some of the former trustees had met after the legislative session of 1815-1816

Signature page from minutes taken at the first meeting of the Board of Visitors of Central College. (Courtesy Special Collections, University of Virginia)

and developed a list of desirable appointees. The six men recommended to the governor by this group consisted of ex-presidents Thomas Jefferson and James Madison, incumbent president James Monroe, and neighboring legislators David Watson of Louisa, Joseph C. Cabell of Nelson, and General John Hartwell Cocke of Fluvanna County. The governor accepted the full slate. Only Jefferson had been a member of the Albemarle Academy board. The addition of the others not only added luster to the new board, but their appointment signified in yet another way that the principal founder of Central College aimed for that institution to be far more than "a petty academy" or just another regional college. Certainly no other college in the state—or in the nation, for that matter—could boast of such a distinguished governing board.[120]

Thomas Jefferson now had legislative approval for his college and a prominent board of visitors in place. He turned next to the challenge of getting that college underway and, to the degree possible, directing events that would enable him to convert Central College into the University of Virginia. That outcome, however, was anything but certain.

Chapter Eight

Bricks, Mortar, and the Politics of Education: From Central College to the University of Virginia

I am now entirely absorbed in endeavors to effect the establishment of a general system of education in my native state ... [encompassing] elementary schools ... collegiate institutions ... [and a] university .... This last establishment will probably be within a mile of Charlottesville and four from Monticello if the system should be adopted at all by our legislature .... My hopes however are kept in check by the ordinary character of our state legislatures, the members of which do not generally possess information enough to perceive the important truths, that knowledge is power, that knowledge is safety, and that knowledge is happiness.

— Thomas Jefferson to George Ticknor, November 25, 1817[121]

Several months after being informed by Governor Nicholas of his appointment to the Board of Visitors of Central College, Joseph Cabell wrote to Jefferson that he stood ready at all times "to attend to any business to which the appointment may give rise." But Cabell's letter also contained words of caution: "I fear it will be difficult, if not impracticable," he said, "to procure money for that institution." Cabell's fear was based upon his awareness that there was at that time renewed discussion in the legislature regarding the development of elementary and secondary schools, as well as talk of establishing a state university. While such interest might have been welcomed, sectional rivalries and competing political philosophies threatened to divide the supporters of education into rival camps, especially with respect to three important issues: (1) How should the lower schools, colleges, and state university be financed? (2) Which should be established first, the lower schools or the university? and (3) In what part of the state should the university, if established, be located? The answers that would be offered by Jefferson and his Central College allies were to be hotly contested by opponents with differing priorities and objectives.

Jefferson was consistently of the opinion that, financially, state efforts should be focused on creating a superior university while encouraging and directing localities to establish and fund lower schools. Cabell warned, however, that the prevailing opinion in the legislature favored using monies in the Literary Fund to establish the lower schools first and institutions of higher learning afterwards. Moreover, Cabell pointedly signaled that in addition to financial difficulties and differences, sectional battles loomed ahead regarding the site for the state university if and when it might be authorized. Existing colleges were expected to weigh in as contenders for university status. William and Mary had its supporters, as did Washington College in Lexington. And, although the little town of Staunton could not offer an operational college as a university base, boosters there had an eye on becoming the capital of the state and believed if they could capture the new university, the likelihood of the capital being relocated from Richmond to that more central site in the Shenandoah Valley would be greatly enhanced. In fact, Cabell informed Jefferson in January of 1817 that "when I was at Staunton, the very spot where the University was to be placed was pointed out to me." Cabell added: "And should there be a bank at Staunton, you may expect to hear it called the *Central* Bank." Jefferson's insistence on "Central" as the name for his embryonic college was thus more than an act of modesty. He had anticipated that the contest over location might in large measure be fought over the issue of centrality and convenience. It was against this backdrop of political strategizing that Jefferson and the Board of Visitors began the task of erecting their little college on the outskirts of Charlottesville in the spring of 1817.[122]

The first meeting of the Board of Visitors of Central College was slated to occur on April 8, 1817, but only two members, Cabell and Cocke, were able to meet with Jefferson at Monticello that day. Lacking a quorum and thus unable to take any official action, they set a next meeting date of May 5 and then adjourned to inspect parcels of land that Jefferson thought might be suitable as a "second best" site for the college. Jefferson had initially looked favorably upon some land closer to town owned by John Kelly, a former member of the Albemarle Academy board. Kelly was apparently disposed to sell the property until he learned that Jefferson was behind the offer to purchase. A Federalist in political leanings and now angry about having been passed over as a member of the new Board of Visitors, Kelly reportedly rejected an offer by abruptly declaring that "I will see him at the devil before he shall have it at any price." Jefferson is said to have remarked: "The man is a fool, but if we cannot get the best site, we must be content with the best we can get."[123]

The best site the visitors could get that would serve their purposes was land owned by John M. Perry that was located "a mile above [west] of the town" and approximately three to four miles west of Monticello. Two sections were under consideration, one consisting of a timbered tract of 153 acres encompassing what would become known as Observatory Mountain and a second of nearly 44 acres that had as its most remarkable feature an impoverished, abandoned field that once had been part of a farm owned by James Monroe. Jefferson envisioned harvesting stone and lumber from the larger site to use in the construction of the college on the smaller one. The portion that would form the college grounds was bordered on the north by the Three Notched Road (the present-day University Avenue), a major route connecting Richmond and the western part of the state, and on the south by Wheeler's Road (now Jefferson Park Avenue). The vista of the Blue Ridge was not as prominent as Jefferson doubtless would have preferred and the irregular slope of the land from north to south would present some problems for adhering to Jefferson's earlier drawings for the layout of buildings around a flat square of grass and trees. Still, determining that Perry's terms for the sale of the land were reasonable and that the lay of the land was "a law of nature to which they were bound to conform," the three board members agreed to purchase both parcels subject to the approval of the full board at a later meeting.[124]

All members of the board except David Watson and Joseph Cabell attended

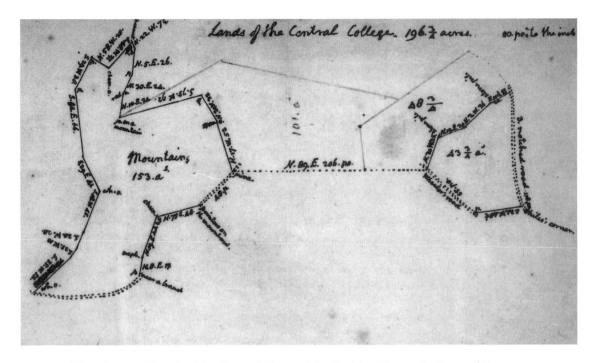

Plat showing "Lands of the Central College," (c. 1819) by Thomas Jefferson. (Courtesy Jefferson Papers, Special Collections, University of Virginia)

the May 5, 1817, meeting. With four members constituting a quorum, the board appointed non-members Valentine W. Southall as secretary and Alexander Garrett as proctor and authorized Garrett to finalize the purchase from Perry for the sum of $1,580.75. The offer of purchase, however, was contingent upon the college being in receipt of the subscriptions and donations that were to be transferred from Albemarle Academy, along with funds from the sale of a portion of the glebe lands that lay within Albemarle County. The glebe lands alone brought in about twice the amount needed to purchase Perry's land. Upon obtaining the transfer of those funds from the now defunct Albemarle Academy, Garrett completed the transaction with Perry in September of 1817. The Board of Visitors of Central College now had possession of two sections of land totaling about two hundred acres that contained a promising, though not perfect, building site within view of Monticello.[125]

The board then approved a lottery and subscription campaign as means to raise additional funds for Central College. Although the lottery scheme was never inaugurated, the subscription campaign yielded encouraging results, especially in Albemarle and closely surrounding counties. Each of the visitors present at the May 5th meeting pledged $1000 toward the campaign, a sum that Jefferson could hardly afford. Cocke took the liberty of volunteering the absent Cabell for the same amount. David Watson, who never seemed much invested in the work of the board and was soon dropped as a member, pledged $200. One hundred twenty-nine citizens of Albemarle County pledged over $27,000 with subscriptions ranging from $20 to $1000. Some of Jefferson's neighbors of more modest means made their contributions in lumber, plaster, bacon, grain, "medical services," or, in the case of James Dinsmore, one of Monticello's master builders who became the chief carpenter on the college project, in labor. In all, over $44,000 in subscriptions were pledged, although not all subscribers met their obligation.[126]

With the land secured and the subscription campaign underway, the board turned its attention to the design and actual construction of the college. The board had no difficulty in determining that the novel campus plan that Jefferson had presented to the Albemarle Academy trustees back in 1814 would do quite nicely as the design for Central College. The visitors directed that construction begin on the first pavilion and its attached dormitories as soon as feasible with an eye toward their completion, "if possible, during the ensuing summer and winter." Jefferson and his colleagues wanted the construction of Central College to be as far along as possible before the convening of the next legislative session at which there would doubtless be discussion regarding establishing a state university at some as yet unspecified location.

Soon after the May 1817 board meeting, Jefferson initiated correspondence with Dr. William Thornton and Benjamin Henry Latrobe regarding the design of the grounds and buildings. Both Thornton and Latrobe were highly regarded architects who had, among other notable projects, worked on design plans for the Capitol in Washington. Although Jefferson was himself an accomplished architect, he had sold his library, including his books on architecture, to Congress in 1815 to replace those burned by British troops during the War of 1812. When the actual work on Central College began in 1817, he did not have at hand the works of Andrea Palladio and others who heretofore had provided him with inspiration and models of classical designs. Jefferson gradually rebuilt his collection of architectural and other books, but now turned to others for advice as well.

In explaining the project to Thornton less than a week after the board decided to commence building, Jefferson provided dimensions for the faculty homes (pavilions) and student rooms and stressed that the pavilions "should be models of taste & good architecture, & of a variety of appearance, no two alike, so as to serve as specimens for the Architectural Lectures." He asked Thornton to "set your imagination to work & sketch some designs for us, no matter how loosely with the pen, without the trouble of referring to scale or rule, for we want nothing but the outline of the architecture, as the internal must be arranged according to local convenience." In both this letter and one of similar nature that he sent to Latrobe on June 12, Jefferson included a rough sketch of the layout of buildings he had presented to the Albemarle Academy board three years earlier.[127]

Replies from Thornton and Latrobe indicated strong approval of Jefferson's basic designs, but both architects also offered suggestions for improvement, some of which Jefferson accepted while others he ignored. Jefferson did not heed Thornton's advice that the dormitory roofs should be slanted rather than flat. However, he did accept that the arcades along the length of the pavilions should not be supported with square pillars as Jefferson had originally specified, but with columns, such as are now in place. Another significant recommendation was that a single Corinthian pavilion should be built on the north side of the square that would make it the most conspicuous structure within the three closed sides of the area that Jefferson began referring to as "the lawn," the area that on many college campuses would be known as a quadrangle.[128]

Latrobe, perhaps the most competent professional architect in the country at the time, carefully studied Jefferson's "entirely novel plan" for the college and on June 28 informed Jefferson that he had derived "so much pleasure" contemplating his sketches that the number of drawings he himself had drafted for pavilions "have grown into a larger bulk than can be conveniently sent by the mail." Latrobe suggested, as had Thornton, increasing the living space allotted the professors in each pavilion and, also like Thornton, recommended placing a structure of imposing character in the middle of the north line. "The centre building ought to exhibit

Detail showing plan for the University of Virginia from letter from Benjamin H. Latrobe to Thomas Jefferson, July 24, 1817. (Courtesy Library of Congress)

in mass and detail as perfect a specimen of good architectural taste as can be devised," advised Latrobe. Jefferson's later decision to use the Pantheon as a model for this "Rotunda" more than fulfilled that objective.[129]

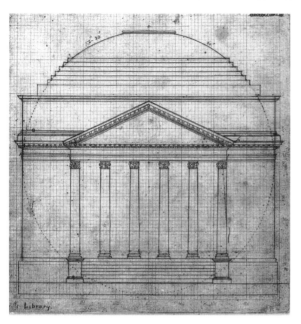

"South Elevation of the Rotunda" (1818-1819) by Thomas Jefferson. (Courtesy Jefferson Papers, Special Collections, University of Virginia)

On July 18 Jefferson surveyed the site of his academical village and laid off three north-south terraces, each 255 feet long, which defined the length of the Lawn. The slope of the land necessitated a design that was rectangular rather than square. He marked the distance between the line of pavilions and dormitory rooms on the east and west sides of the Lawn at 200 feet. The day after Jefferson surveyed the Lawn, he wrote to General Cocke to inform him that "our squares are laid off, the brickyard begun, and the leveling will be begun in the course of the week."

Jefferson requested that Cocke join him to look over the grounds later in the month and then go with him to Madison's home, Montpelier, in nearby Orange County, to conduct pressing business of the board. With Cabell also in attendance to make a quorum, the four visitors met on July 28, approving the design for the first planned pavilion (Pavilion VII) and authorizing Jefferson to take measures to hire a stone-cutter from Italy.[130]

As construction began on the first pavilion, the task of flattening and terracing the surface of the Lawn was assigned to ten men, most likely hired slaves, who worked during the summer and fall with shovels and hoes to shape the land to Jefferson's specifications. John Perry, who had sold the land to the visitors, was given the contract for erecting Pavilion VII, the present-day Colonnade Club. Plans for a cornerstone-laying ceremony were set in motion, and the event was slated for "Court Day," October 6, 1817. When the day arrived, the county and

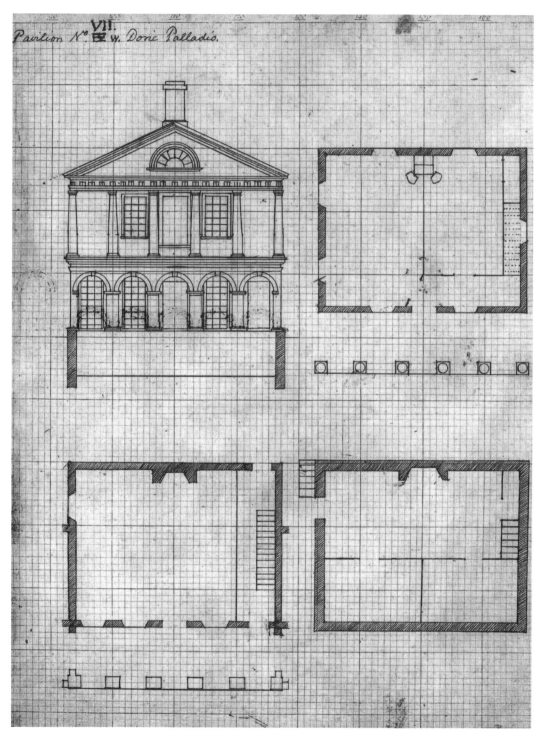

"Study for Pavilion VII" (1817) by Thomas Jefferson. (Courtesy Jefferson Papers, Special Collections, University of Virginia)

superior court judges left their benches and joined the parade of citizens that made its way to the college grounds. Masons from Lodges 60 and 90 officiated at the cornerstone-laying ceremony, but the attention of most of the citizens must have been fixed on the two former presidents of the United States, Jefferson and Madison, and the current president, James Monroe, whose presence as members of the Board of Visitors added special dignity and excitement to the occasion. Historian Philip A. Bruce described a portion of the scene as follows: "President Monroe applied the square and plumb, the chaplain asked a blessing on the stone, the crowd huzzaed, and the band played 'Hail Columbia.' " As part of the Masonic ceremony, "corn was now scattered, and then Valentine W. Southall delivered the address to the general audience. With the grand-master's address to the Visitors, the ceremony was concluded." The construction of Central College was officially underway.[131]

Even before the ground had been broken for the first pavilion, the visitors had begun giving consideration to recruiting a faculty for their new college. Jefferson noted in the minutes of the visitors for July 28, 1817, that the board agreed to make an overture to the Rev. Dr. Samuel Knox of Baltimore to be the first professor for Central College. Knox, whose essay on the best mode of education for the United States had been judged by the American Philosophical Society as prize-worthy in 1797, was thought to be a promising candidate for the professorship of languages, belles lettres, rhetoric, history, and geography. The board agreed that his salary would be $500, supplemented by $25 from every student who enrolled in his classes. He was, of course, also to be provided with a pavilion.[132]

When the visitors later received word, prematurely as it turned out, that Knox had retired "from the business of instructing youths," they turned their attention to other candidates. At a meeting on the day following the cornerstone-laying ceremony, the board extended an invitation to Dr. Thomas Cooper to become professor of law and chemistry. Cooper, it will be recalled, was Joseph Priestley's son-in-law who had long been admired by Jefferson and was among those to whom Jefferson had turned for advice on his university plans. An outspoken critic of Federalism, Cooper had been sentenced to a short jail term for violation of the Alien and Sedition Acts during the administration of John Adams, but with the coming of the "Revolution of 1800" and Jefferson's election, his political fortunes changed and he was appointed to a judgeship in Pennsylvania. A month before the board tendered its offer to Cooper, Jefferson had written him describing in broad terms his plans for Central College. Jefferson suggested that Cooper would be the ideal candidate for a professorship in chemistry, zoology, botany, mineralogy, and anatomy and that law could be added to his professorship "because that will draw to it many students & make it very profitable." Jefferson proposed, and the board later approved, a salary for Cooper of $1000 plus tuition fees of $20 from each of his students. Stating that his aim was to make "this seminary the first in the Union," Jefferson also assured Cooper that professorships, once established, would be permanent and that interest off funds deposited would be sufficient to "pay his salary forever." Whether Cooper merited it or not, it is obvious that Jefferson held him in high esteem.[133]

Cooper's candidacy for a professorship was in startling contrast to Knox's. While Knox was a liberal Presbyterian clergyman, Cooper was considered by many to be an atheist, although he sometimes contended "Unitarian" was a more appropriate appellation for one holding his beliefs—or disbeliefs. Jefferson admired Cooper for his scientific researches, unorthodox religious beliefs, and strong Republican loyalties, but Joseph Cabell tended to agree with the widely held view that Cooper was "defective" in manners, habits, or character and was "certainly rather unpopular in the enlightened part of society." Cabell considered an invitation to Cooper to be a matter of "great delicacy" and urged Jefferson to pause and reconsider the implications of offering Cooper a professorship. Enemies of the institution, Cabell warned, would seize upon Cooper's appointment as another occasion to "keep it down." Although Cabell was proven correct, as will be discussed more fully in the concluding chapter, Jefferson refused to back away from this candidate, a decision that one historian termed "the biggest mistake [Jefferson] made in founding the university."[134]

While Cooper mulled over the prospects of moving to Virginia and the Board of Visitors uneasily awaited his answer, Jefferson had to concentrate his attention on other matters. His campaign to capture the University of Virginia for Charlottesville required him not only to oversee the funding and construction of buildings and try to lure a faculty of the first order to his fledgling college, but to struggle as well with members of the state legislature who were mapping strategies and pursuing objectives of a different sort. Jefferson had to do battle on two fronts, one in Charlottesville and the other in Richmond. Charging ahead with efforts to turn Albemarle red clay into bricks and buildings for Central College, he was at the same time deploying Cabell and his troops into position to engage in legislative fights in order to capture the main prize, the University of Virginia.

All the while that Jefferson and his co-laborers were pushing to give their college actual form and substance, the Virginia legislature was giving increasingly serious attention to educational measures that held promise of creating a statewide system of schools and perhaps a capstone university. Enthusiasm for schools had become more contagious as the result of a promised loan repayment to the state by the federal government. During the War of 1812, Virginia had loaned money to the United States government to assist in the prosecution of the war and had incurred additional expenses for its own defense. Both amounts were reimbursable at war's end. After hostilities had ceased and payment came due, there was general agreement that the surplus of the federal subsidy should be placed in Virginia's Literary Fund. Projections held that this addition to the Literary Fund would increase the Fund's value by nearly $1,000,000 by the end of 1817.[135]

Delegate Charles Fenton Mercer of Loudoun County, who had played a key role in the establishment of the Literary Fund in 1810, emerged again to take up the cause of education. As chairman of the House Committee on Finance, Mercer was in a strategic position to influence state appropriations. Moreover, Mercer was recognized as a leader of the faction that sought more recognition and power for the growing numbers of Virginians who were populating regions west of the Blue Ridge and into and beyond the Allegheny Mountains.

Upon hearing in early 1816 that Mercer was contemplating a proposal to appropriate a considerable part of the swollen Literary Fund proceeds toward the promotion of "a grand scheme" of education, Cabell shared with him a copy of Jefferson's 1814 letter to Peter Carr. Cabell informed Jefferson on January 24, 1816, just three weeks before the Central College bill received legislative approval, that Mercer seemed "much pleased with your view on the subject" and that both he and Mercer thought that Jefferson's letter should be published in the *Enquirer*, Richmond's leading newspaper, thus giving Jefferson's ideas wider circulation. Sensing the need to move quickly, Cabell submitted the letter to the *Enquirer* even before Jefferson gave permission for him to do so. Moreover, aware that Mercer would favor a western site for the university, Cabell reasoned that location was a "secondary condition" and that he could support Mercer's education funding proposal in hopes that the question of fixing the site for the university might be dealt with separately. "Appropriations abstracted from their location are most easily obtained," Cabell later explained to Jefferson. Of course, to both Mercer and Jefferson, location was far from being a secondary consideration. That issue, however, was not addressed when the legislature approved Mercer's resolution that specified that, after other obligations were met, the remaining large portion of the federal debt repayment sum was to be placed in the Literary Fund for expenditures on public education. Indeed, Cabell took satisfaction in the belief that the printing of Jefferson's letter to Carr in the *Enquirer* "had a considerable effect in promoting the passage of that resolution."[136]

Both the act establishing Central College and the Mercer resolution were passed during the month of February 1816, the former on the 14th and the latter on the 24th. Cabell reported to Jefferson that, in accepting Mercer's resolution, the legislature had also required the president and directors of the Literary Fund "to report to the next Assembly the best plan of a university, colleges, academies, and schools." The resolution stipulated that the report should provide for "the establishment of one University, to be called 'The University of Virginia,'" along with such additional colleges, academies, and schools as would be needed to "diffuse the benefits of education throughout the Commonwealth." This resolution marked the legislature's first official sanction for bringing into existence a University of Virginia.[137]

Cabell was well aware of the threat posed by legislators who favored a western site and who were prepared to divide the state if the university were not placed beyond the Blue Ridge. "Staunton wants the seat of government, and considers the day near at hand, when she will be the metropolis of the State," Cabell advised Jefferson, while Washington College in Lexington "will be the favorite of the Federalists." Still, Cabell wrote encouragingly (if not altogether convincingly): "I think the Central College will triumph over them all." Cabell—and Jefferson— were pinning their hopes on gaining seats for more allies in the coming election and on the fact that the governor of the state, Wilson C. Nicholas, who had supported Jefferson's educational aspirations in the past, would continue to do so.[138]

Jefferson's confidence in the governor seemed well placed. Nicholas, in his capacity as president of the Literary Fund, turned immediately to Jefferson for advice. Jefferson responded in a lengthy letter composed at Monticello on April 2, 1816. Jefferson directed Nicholas's attention to the similarity between the legislature's rather general call for an outline for a publicly funded school system and his own more specific provisions in his 1779 Bill for the More General Diffusion of Knowledge and his 1814 letter to Peter Carr. The best arrangement of courses at the various levels, the proper "village" layout of buildings for the university, and the merits of the division of counties into wards for the support and supervision of elementary schools were all again reviewed by Jefferson. He concluded his recommendations by telling the governor that, "should the board of directors [of the Literary Fund] approve of the plan and make ward divisions the substratum of their elementary schools, their report may furnish a happy occasion of introducing them."[139]

However satisfied Nicholas may have been with Jefferson's recommendations, he was obligated to collect information from a variety of knowledgeable consultants. On May 30, 1816, Governor Nicholas issued a circular letter to "sundry gentlemen on the subject of public education for the state of Virginia." Among those from whom advice was solicited were James Monroe (then secretary of state under Madison), Dr. Thomas Cooper (at the time professor of chemistry at Carlyle College), Dr. J. Augustine Smith (president of William and Mary), Rev. Timothy Dwight (president of Yale), and Dr. Samuel L. Mitchell of New York. Smith was noticeably silent on the matter of university education while Cooper, in good Jeffersonian style, volunteered that "*Universities* should be exclusively for a liberal and finished education. I doubt whether it would be expedient to have more than one in the State, under State patronage." Dwight pointed out that there was a great deal of confusion in America regarding the terms "college" and "university," while

Mitchell focused on New York's statewide system of public education. Monroe tactfully held back from giving advice, noting that there were others in Virginia more knowledgeable than he on the subject.[140]

The "Report and Digest of the President and Directors of the Literary Fund" was finally submitted to the legislature on December 6, 1816. In summarizing the report, historian Herbert B. Adams observed that "The official voice is the Governor's, but the hand is Jefferson's." From the subdivision of counties into townships within which were to be elementary schools, through academies in which provision would be made for "the boys of brightest genius," and on to a university that would comprehend "the whole circle of the arts and sciences" and extend "to the utmost boundaries of human knowledge," the Literary Fund's report to the General Assembly reflected many ideas and elements of plans long advocated by Thomas Jefferson.[141]

There were two critical points of difference, however, between the Literary Fund report and Jefferson's philosophy, differences that prompted another historian, Roy Honeywell, to conclude that the report "seems to have been very little influenced by Jefferson." Seeing the surplus monies in the Literary Fund as a way to avoid placing a distasteful and "burdensome" tax on the citizenry, the report proposed applying existing state funds toward the inauguration and support of the system of public schools. Moreover, the Literary Fund report raised the question as to "whether it would not be better to execute the system by degrees" beginning with the elementary schools and working upward toward a university. This would leave the university subject to development *only* if a surplus remained after funding the elementary and secondary schools of the Commonwealth. While Jefferson had consistently advocated erecting a complete system and considered elementary and secondary schools as absolutely essential, he had also insisted that localities assume the responsibility for funding the lower schools and, especially in his retirement years, directed most of his energy toward bringing into existence the university. An indication of the depth of Jefferson's belief that localities rather than the state should superintend and finance local schools is revealed in a letter that he wrote to Cabell almost a year before the Literary Fund report had been submitted: "... [I]f it is believed that these elementary schools will be better managed by the Governor and Council, the Commissioners of the Literary Fund, or any other general authority of the Government, than by the parents within each ward, it is a belief against all experience …. No, my friend, the way to have good and safe government, is not to trust it all to one; but to divide it among the many, distributing to every one exactly the functions he is competent to."[142]

The "Report and Digest" submitted by the Literary Fund directors was obviously the result of debate and compromise. More debate and attempts at compromise followed over the ensuing months. Mercer attempted to make the matter of state funding more palatable by proposing a scheme to augment the Literary Fund through the establishment of a system of "State Literary Fund Banks," from which interest proceeds would supposedly double the amount of money available within four years. This measure was hotly criticized by Jeffersonian Republicans and was defeated by a narrow vote in the Senate even though it had overwhelming support in the House. Other bills and amendments confounded deliberations during the 1816-17 General Assembly session. Proposals and counterproposals, agitated by a frenzy of newspaper editorials and letters, many of which were orchestrated by Jefferson, Cabell, and their allies on one side and Mercer forces on the other, led to a stalemate. Thomas Ritchie, editor of the Richmond *Enquirer*, summarized the results of that legislative session by observing: "Let the truth be told. They spent much time in doing very little good …. They have attempted to do many things which finally ended in smoke."[143]

The next session of the legislature that opened in December 1817 proved to be just as contentious as the previous one. The fundamental differences separating the Mercer forces that dominated the House and the Cabell-Jefferson forces that had an edge in the Senate were again brought to the fore. Mercer introduced a bill to establish a university, four colleges (in addition to incorporating into the system William and Mary, Washington, and Hampden-Sydney colleges—and ignoring Central College), forty-eight academies (to include existing private schools, including several for girls), and primary schools dispersed throughout the state, *all* supported by the Literary Fund. Jefferson complained to Cabell that Mercer's plan would "exhaust the whole funds" in establishing the primary schools alone and that a university "would never come into question." If the financial arrangements in Mercer's bill were not troublesome enough, his provision that the new state university be located "at some place between the Blue Ridge and the Alleghany mountains" surely provoked Jefferson's ire.[144]

Having anticipated the legislative battles ahead, Jefferson had prepared in the previous September a bill for establishing elementary schools "without taking a cent from the Literary Fund." At Cabell's suggestion, he merged this bill into a more comprehensive one in October that detailed a somewhat revised version of his earlier hierarchical system. Adjustments and refinements were needed, he wrote to another correspondent, to make the system accommodate "to the circumstances of this day" rather than those of an earlier time. Tax-supported elementary schools offering free instruction to children of all citizens in every ward still formed the basis of his proposed system. At the intermediate level, Jefferson now proposed the creation of a Board of Public Instruction and the division of the state into nine collegiate districts. This body was to appoint a board of visitors for each new college that would be constructed in each district. Not wanting to give aid to existing colleges that would be rivals with his Charlottesville institution for selection as the University of Virginia, he did not propose bringing them or Central College into the state system. Each of the nine new colleges, in addition to courses in the basic humanities and mathematics, would offer instruction in French, Italian, Spanish, and German as well as Latin and Greek. By dividing the state into nine collegiate districts instead of the twenty grammar school districts called for in his 1779 plan, Jefferson's 1817 plan economized by reducing both the number of institutions and number of students who would be provided scholarships for university study, but the principle of providing for the advancement of gifted students from the intermediate levels through the university was maintained.[145]

While Jefferson cautioned Cabell that it would be best if he were not known to be the author of these bills and disingenuously stated that he wanted it understood "that I do not intermeddle with public affairs," meddle he did! Not only was he behind the education bill introduced by Cabell in January 1818, but he also took it upon himself to send a report on the progress of Central College to the legislature in the same month. There was no requirement or even expectation that any sort of report on what the legislature considered a local college should be forthcoming. Jefferson, however, intended to use the report, which he addressed to the Speaker of the House of Delegates, for propaganda purposes. Clearly, no small part of his objective was to persuade the legislature (and, given that the item was subsequently published in the *Enquirer*, the entire state) that Central College was indeed far more than a local institution. Using the rationale that Central College was in a sense a public institution under the patronage of the governor who was empowered to appoint its board of visitors, Jefferson and the other visitors, all of whom signed the report, alleged to "deem it our duty to report to you our proceedings under that appointment." Jefferson described the architectural design that allowed for expansion, the progress of the subscription campaign and construction, the measures underway to recruit faculty, and the salubrious climate and convenient location of the college. As he concluded the report, he unabashedly offered Central College to the state of Virginia as the logical foundation for its anticipated university. "[W]e are so certain of the approbation of those for whom we act," Jefferson had written, "that we may give safe assurance of the ready transfer to the State of all the property and rights of the Central College ... towards the establishment of ... a University."[146]

Despite the strategies and maneuvering by Mercer, Cabell, Jefferson, and others who chose sides according to the sometimes fixed, sometimes shifting, political, sectional, religious, and educational positions of the day, neither side won a victory. On January 23, 1818, Cabell informed Jefferson that "the prospect before us is dreary," and on February 1, he wrote again that "I totally despair of the success of any general plan whatsoever." When a vote was taken on Jefferson's bill in the House of Delegates on February 11, Cabell's fears were confirmed. "It received very few votes," Cabell informed Jefferson, and noted that a substitute bill replacing all previous education bills was then introduced by Delegate Hill of King William County and had been approved. Hill's bill made no mention of academies, colleges, or a university, but rather provided for an appropriation of $45,000 from the Literary Fund to establish schools in every county for children of the poor. When the bill reached the Senate on February 19, it was adopted by a wide margin. The bill was signed into law on February 21, 1818.[147]

This provision for charity schools proved disappointing to many. Thomas

Ritchie editorialized in the *Enquirer* that "we want schools for teaching the higher branches, we want men who can do more than read, write and cipher .... [L]et us assist the poor, but *let us do more*, let us assist the genius of our countrymen." Surely Jefferson and Cabell were disappointed as well, but Cabell did manage to engraft a rider on the Senate version that proved to be tremendously significant. Cabell's amendment specified that $15,000 should be set aside annually toward the support of a university. The final version of the bill that became an Act Appropriating Part of the Revenue of the Literary Fund and for Other Purposes left open the question of location. The act called for the appointment of a commission of "twenty-four discreet and intelligent persons," one from each senatorial district, to determine for the university a proper site, a building plan, curriculum, number and description of professorships, and mode of governance. Cabell's amendment, piggybacked on a bill providing for the education of the poor, gave renewed life to the possibility of salvaging Jefferson's dream of founding the University of Virginia. The fate of the university now rested in large measure on decisions to be made by commissioners who were to meet at a tavern in the Blue Ridge Mountains late in the following summer. The inn at Rockfish Gap on Afton Mountain would provide a geographically neutral zone for deliberations along with cool breezes during the hot days of August.

REPORT

OF THE

COMMISSIONERS

FOR THE

UNIVERSITY OF VIRGINIA,

ASSEMBLED AT ROCK-FISH GAP, IN THE COUNTY

OF AUGUSTA, AUGUST

CHARLOTTESVILL[E]

PRINTED BY C. P. M'[KENNIE]

::::::::::::::

1824.

Title page and page one of the Rockfish Gap Report. (Courtesy Special Collections, University of Virginia)

REPORT.

The Commissioners of the University of Virginia, having met as by law required, at the Tavern in Rockfish Gap on the Blue Ridge, on the first day of August of this present year 1818, and having formed a board proceeded on that day to the discharge of the duties assigned to them by the Act of the Legislature entituled an "Act appropriating part of the Literary Fund, and for other purposes," and having continued their proceedings by adjournment from day to day, to Tuesday the fourth day of August, have agreed to a report on the several matters with which they were charged, which report they now respectfully address and submit to the Legislature of the State.

The first duty enjoined on them was to enquire and report a site in some convenient and proper part of the State, for an University, to be called the "University of Virginia."

In this enquiry they supposed that the governing considerations should be the healthiness of the site, the fertility of the neighbouring country, and its centrality to the white population of the whole State: for, although the Act authorised and required them to receive any voluntary contributions, whether conditional or absolute, which might be offered through them to the President and Directors of the Literary Fund, for the benefit of the University, yet they did not consider this as establishing an auction, or as pledging the location to the highest bidder.

Three places were proposed; to wit, Lexington in the County of Rockbridge, Staunton in the County of Augusta, and the Central College, in the County of Albemarle: each of these was unexceptionable as to healthiness and fertility. It was the degree of centrality to the white population of the State which alone then constituted the important point of comparison between these places; and the Board, after full enquiry, and impartial and mature consideration, are of opinion that the central point of the white population of the State is nearer to the Central College, than to either Lexington, or Staunton, by great and important differences; and

Chapter Nine

Jefferson's "Last Act of Usefulness": The Founding of the University of Virginia

*I have long been sensible that while I was endeavoring to render our coun-
try the greatest of all services, that of regenerating the public education,
and placing our rising generation on the level of our sister States (which
they have proudly held heretofore), I was discharging the odious function
of a physician pouring medicine down the throat of a patient insensible of
needing it. I am so sure of the future approbation of posterity, and of the
inestimable effect we shall have produced in the elevation of our country by
what we have done, as that I cannot repent of the part I have borne ....*

— Thomas Jefferson to Joseph C. Cabell,
February 7, 1826[148]

During the 1817-18 legislative battles that pitted Jefferson's allies led by
Cabell against the pro-western and Federalist forces of Charles F. Mercer, Jefferson
had written to his former treasury secretary, Albert Gallatin, that his educational
hopes for Virginia were being countered by "ignorance, malice, egoism," political
and religious "fanaticism," and "local perversities." While Jefferson's frustration
was understandable and his complaints not far from the mark, there was more
to the matter than that. There is no question but that Jefferson himself was the
source of much opposition. In a letter to fellow visitor James Madison, Joseph
Cabell delicately laid out the dynamics of the moment as well as any friend and
confidant could. Cabell explained to Madison that, while the delegates beyond the
Blue Ridge were divided among themselves as to whether Staunton or Lexington

should become the site for the university, "they unite as one body against us." Their fear, Cabell contended, was that the supporters of the Central College site themselves had designs on making Charlottesville the future capital of the state. Moreover, he noted, Jefferson's religious opinions caused the Presbyterian clergy (and others) to be "very hostile" to any project with which he was associated. Cabell continued, "The Federalists view it [Central College] with a malignant eye. The friends of William and Mary regard it as a future rival. You are doubtless apprized of the hostility of certain persons in the county of Albemarle to Mr. Jefferson and his friends. These persons have contrived to communicate their prejudices to some members from some of the other counties in the middle country .... The friends of Rockbridge College [Washington College], perceiving the state of things, have profited of it to alienate these persons from the Central College, and to draw them into their interests. Added to all, the House of Delegates is lamentably deficient in abilities." Cabell concluded by admitting to Madison that "this combination of unfortunate circumstances" was defeating their expectations and had thrown both Jefferson and Cabell "into utter despair."[149]

The passage in February 1818 of the charity school bill with Cabell's accompanying university amendment cast a ray of light into the cloud of despair that had hovered over the Central College visitors during much of the winter of 1818. Intent on trying to use his senatorial influence to the fullest extent possible, Cabell immediately asked Jefferson if he would consider representing their district on the commission that would be appointed by the governor, if that could be arranged. Jefferson's reply, while not closing the door to his appointment, clearly revealed that he was quite aware of the animosity many felt for him. Agreeing with Cabell that Madison should be persuaded to represent their neighboring district on the commission, Jefferson hesitated regarding his own role in future negotiations on behalf of Central College. "As for myself," he wrote to Cabell, "I should be ready to do anything in my power for the institution: but that is not the exact question." Jefferson then laid bare the key concern: "Would it promote the success of the institution most for me to be in or out of it? Out of it, I believe. It is still to depend ultimately on the will of the Legislature; and that has its uncertainties. There are fanatics both in religion and politics, who, without knowing me personally, have long been taught to consider me as a raw head and bloody bones, and as we can afford to lose no votes in that body, I do think it would be better that you should be named for our district. Do not consider this as mock-modesty; it is the cool and deliberate act of my judgment. I believe the institution would be more popular without me than with me; and this is the most important consideration." Jefferson closed his letter by advising Cabell to "act on this subject without any scruples as to me or yourself. Regard nothing but the good of the cause."[150]

Cabell had a direct hand in determining what was "good for the cause." In drafting the amendment to Delegate Hill's charity school bill, Cabell had specified that the governor make the appointments to the commission. The incumbent in that office was James Preston, a native of Montgomery County who had become a resident of Albemarle. Preston, although not personally acquainted with his illustrious neighbor, could be presumed to look favorably upon appointees who were likely to support Jefferson's project or who were at least not openly hostile to his ambitions. "The Executive, I think, will do us justice," Cabell confided to Jefferson. Moreover, in providing that each senatorial district be represented, Cabell's rider had loaded the committee with Piedmont and eastern delegates. Fifteen of the twenty-four members of the "Rockfish Gap Commission," as it came to be called, were from senatorial districts east of the Blue Ridge. Finally, in his efforts to arrange appointments to the commission, Cabell and some of his associates conferred and recommended candidates "to a member of the Executive." Citing reasons similar to Jefferson's, Cabell asked that he not be appointed and thought that Jefferson, on the basis of the reasons he himself had cited, might not be selected as well. Nonetheless, Cabell wrote to Jefferson that he had left the matter in the hands of "four or five of your intelligent friends." Those friends apparently were persuaded—and so informed Governor Preston—that the advantages of Jefferson's membership on the commission outweighed the disadvantages he had acknowledged. Jefferson subsequently agreed to join Madison and twenty-two other delegates appointed to the commission, a number of whom had already either cast their lot with Central College as subscribers or had relatives who had done so. Meanwhile, looking beyond the report to be issued by the commission, Cabell invested himself heavily over the next several months in trying to line up candidates for the next legislature who would be favorable to Central College. The commission's recommendation, after all, would be just that, a recommendation. The final outcome would depend upon the disposition of the legislature.[151]

The 1818 act that created the "Board of Commissioners for the University" had directed that the commissioners meet on August 1 at the tavern at Rockfish Gap and then "from time to time and place to place until their duties shall have been performed." Thomas Jefferson, now age seventy-five, took two days to make the journey by horseback from Monticello to the tavern atop Afton Mountain, a distance of around thirty miles. He sent his mattress and other belongings ahead by wagon and divided his journey by resting for the night at the home of George Divers, a friend whose home at Farmington was just a few miles west of Charlottesville. Accompanied by Madison, Jefferson completed the journey the following day.[152]

Three commissioners who had been appointed from Tidewater Virginia did not make the long trip to Rockfish Gap, perhaps believing that William and Mary, whether it remained in Williamsburg or might be moved to Richmond, as some had long been suggesting, had little chance of being selected as the state university. The twenty-one other delegates assembled on Saturday morning, August 1, in the dining room of the inn. The low-ceilinged, white-washed room was furnished with a long, rough table and split-bottom chairs, doubtless worn from years of use. Jefferson was promptly elected to preside over the proceedings. As the deliberations got underway, a committee of six, headed by Jefferson and Madison, was appointed to report on all the matters before the commission except the most controversial one, that of location. Jefferson had conferred with Madison well prior to the meeting and had a report ready-made for study over the weekend by the other four members of the subcommittee.[153]

The main item of business to be discussed was that of location. While all the delegates certainly knew of Jefferson's hopes for Central College and many were predisposed to offer him support, there were some among those assembled who advanced the claims of the more western sites. In terms of assets that might enter into the location decision, the contest was clearly between Washington College and Central College. Those advocates of establishing a new university in

Staunton could offer only promises and ambitions, not buildings and endowments. However, proponents of Washington College, initially chartered in 1782 as Liberty Hall Academy, had considerable inducements that made that option look attractive. The trustees of the Lexington institution proposed transferring one hundred shares of stock in the James River Company, their college's thirty-one acre campus and buildings, the anticipated interest due from an endowment established by the Cincinnati Society, two well-stocked libraries belonging to literary societies, and several thousand dollars in cash. Lexington citizens had pledged an additional $17,878. Even more enticing were lands, slaves, and other possessions valued at approximately $100,000 to be willed to the institution upon the death of John Robinson, a local citizen and college benefactor—*if* Washington College were selected as the site for the university.[154]

Central College, of course, was also prepared to make a handsome offer. Its ante consisted of two hundred acres of property, a completed pavilion with attached dormitories and another under construction, proceeds from the sale of glebe lands, and over $41,000 in subscriptions (not all of which had been collected, however). Cabell secured the permission of every subscriber permitting the visitors to transfer the property of the college to the commonwealth if that site were chosen for the university. By the time of the Rockfish Gap meeting, the visitors had already executed and recorded in the clerk's office of Albemarle County a deed transferring these properties to the Literary Fund, contingent upon the decision regarding site.[155]

After spokesmen for Lexington and Staunton had made their appeals, Jefferson presented his brief for Central College. According to Judge John G. Jackson, one of the commissioners from the western region, Jefferson moderated the meeting with a fair and even hand and showed no preference of any sort until it became his time to speak. When he did take the floor, Jefferson pulled from his belongings a map of Virginia that he proceeded to spread out before the commissioners. Jefferson pointed to a line he had drawn running from the mouth of the Chesapeake Bay through Charlottesville, Rockfish Gap, and Staunton on to the Ohio River. He explained that his calculations, based on the 1810 census and information he had collected during the summer from every court clerk in Virginia, showed that this east-west line split the state evenly with a difference of only fifteen thousand white citizens north or south of that line. A similar east-west line running through Lexington to the Ohio River revealed an excess of over ninety-one thousand residing north of that division. Clearly, he contended, Charlottesville and Staunton were more centrally located with respect to the distribution of the state's white population than was Lexington.

North-south divisions running through each of the sites also favored the Charlottesville location. Jefferson's lines and figures indicated that the Central College campus was more equidistant from the North Carolina border to the south and the Potomac River boundary to the north than either of the other two sites. Jefferson then explained lines on the map that ran on a slant from northeast to southwest along either side of the Blue Ridge mountain range, a "natural" dividing line. With numbers plotted on the map, Jefferson instructed his colleagues that the distribution of the white population was centered much more closely to Charlottesville than to either of the other sites west of the Blue Ridge. As if to clinch the deal, so at least tradition has it, Jefferson then reportedly drew from his bags a sheaf of papers bearing a long list of names. The names, Jefferson is said to have explained, were those of every citizen of Albemarle County who had reached the age of eighty. The implication was clear: not only was the location the most central, it was the healthiest spot in the state as well![156]

Although the decision on location was doubtlessly settled following Jefferson's presentation, the vote on the matter was not taken until two days following. When the official tally was taken on Monday, three delegates cast their vote for Washington College, two for Staunton, and sixteen for Central College. When discussion turned to matters of the university's curriculum, mode of organization and governance, building design, and other matters that had been assigned to Jefferson's subcommittee, his previously prepared report was, with only minor amendments, quickly adopted by the commission. One final resolution was unanimously adopted before two copies of the report were signed by all twenty-one commissioners the following day: "That the thanks of this board be given to Thomas Jefferson, Esq., for the great ability, impartiality, and dignity, with which he has presided over its deliberations."[157]

Satisfied with the work of the Rockfish Gap Commission, Jefferson, accompanied by two of the commissioners who had initially opposed Central College as the preferred site, rode westward from Rockfish Gap into the Shenandoah Valley. Jefferson had been invited to spend some time in Staunton as a guest of Judge Archibald Stuart, one of the two delegates who had voted for that place as the preferred university site. Jefferson then rode on to Warm Springs in the pleasant company of General James Breckenridge, a delegate who had voted for Lexington. Jefferson did not make the journey westward to mend fences, however, for there was no need. Rather, he hoped the baths at the Springs would ease the pain of his rheumatism. As it turned out, he developed boils on his "seat" and had great difficulty making his way back to Charlottesville several weeks later. When he did finally reach Monticello, he did not mount a horse for several months afterward and did most of his correspondence for a lengthy time thereafter writing in a reclining position.[158]

Jefferson's capable ally, Cabell, was in even more distress during the fall of 1818. He spent most of October confined to his bed, and during an attempt to visit Jefferson in November, he suffered a relapse. Still, Jefferson looked to him to press the battle for the University of Virginia with the legislature. Jefferson entrusted Cabell with the task of taking copies of the Rockfish Gap Report to a printer in Richmond and then presenting printed copies to the Speakers of the House and Senate. The report was received "with great attention" in both houses on December 8, so much so that Cabell wrote to Jefferson that "present prospects are very favorable to a successful issue." By December 14, however, Cabell began expressing concerns to Jefferson. Although Jefferson's masterful display with the Virginia map and its intersecting lines and notations had captivated the delegates at Rockfish Gap, members of the legislature who favored Lexington and who had more time to reflect on the matter were not inclined to accept without further question Jefferson's statistical reasoning. Cabell informed Jefferson that there would be a move to strike Central College from the report, that there was a "party in the House of Delegates opposed to the measure in every shape," and that "the effect of intrigue and management is beyond the reach of calculation." A few days later Cabell confessed that "I am really fearful for the ultimate fate of the bill."

Cabell had become aware that western delegates, unhappy over the location issue, were threatening to combine with eastern delegates, who wanted to abolish the Literary Fund, in order to defeat the bill entirely. Nonetheless, in a follow-up letter the same day, Cabell tried to reassure Jefferson that he would do everything he could to advance their cause, health permitting: "Even if the danger to my life existed, which they [Cabell's worried friends] apprehended, I could not risk it for a better cause."[159]

In a Christmas Eve letter to Jefferson while the legislature was in recess, Cabell told Jefferson that "the party opposed altogether to the University is growing so rapidly, we have just grounds to fear a total failure of the measure." He explained that some adherents to the doctrines of Adam Smith and Dugald Stewart argued that education should not be undertaken by government but should be left to private enterprise. Others complained that the Literary Fund was established for the poor and that the university advocates were diverting the funds from their intended purpose. Still others were contending that the town of Charlottesville was too small and isolated to "furnish polished society for the students" and draw to it capable professors. Moreover, there remained those who questioned Jefferson's calculations of population and geography. On this last issue, Cabell pleaded to Jefferson to send him additional information regarding his statistics and lines of division so that he might be able to present a reasoned argument to questioners.[160]

On New Year's Day, Jefferson composed a reply to the string of anxious letters he had received from Cabell in the preceding weeks. In taking up one point raised by Cabell, that of selecting the mouth of Chesapeake as the point of origin for his east-west division lines, Jefferson admitted that those who complained that this point was more to the south than the midpoint of the state were correct, but, he explained, "the greatest part of what is north is water. There is more land on the south than north." In explaining the lines that ran parallel to the Blue Ridge, the Sage observed that the mountains were a "natural" dividing line and that, since the state was triangular, each half should be so. After providing answers to various challenges to his measurements, he stated: "[R]un your lines in what direction you please, they will pass close to Charlottesville, and for the very good reason that it is truly central to the white population." With a bit of exasperation, Jefferson then noted: "However, let those who wish to set up other lines in competition, make their own calculations. It is a very laborious business. Mine took me two or three days."[161]

Cabell, in spite of his low spirits and poor health (that included bouts of hemorrhaging and coughing blood), did his best to mount a counterattack against the opposition. He persuaded friends to submit letters to the *Enquirer* in support of the university plan and worked far into the night conversing with colleagues on strategies that might insure the success of Jefferson's agenda. His efforts and those of allies began to pay off. He wrote on January 18 that he was "Grateful, truly grateful" to report that the tide was turning and that a motion in the House to strike Central College from the bill had been defeated by a vote of 114 to 69. After the vote was announced, Delegate Briscoe G. Baldwin from Augusta County, of which Staunton was the county seat, rose and made a stirring appeal for the western delegates to put aside regional prejudice and rally to the aid of the university in Charlottesville. Baldwin's passionate speech and evidence of magnanimity on the part of a "defeated adversary" moved some to tears and brought applause from the floor of the House. The vote taken the following day, January 19, revealed only 28 dissenting votes out of a body of 169 members.[162]

On January 25, Cabell steered the bill through the Senate, even though internal bleeding forced him to excuse himself from the proceedings several times. An attempt to strike Central College was again made and turned back. The Senate then approved the bill by a vote of 22 to 1. Cabell's efforts and Jefferson's persistence in pressing for the transforming of Central College into the University of Virginia had paid off—at least in terms of having finally gained legislative authorization. When the governor promptly appointed a new Board of Visitors, the way was cleared for official action. Four of the former members were retained on the board: Jefferson, Madison, Cabell, and John H. Cocke. The governor made the group more representative by the appointment of two men from the western region, Chapman Johnson of Staunton and James Breckenridge of Botetourt County, and one from the Tidewater, General Robert B. Taylor of Norfolk. When the board had its first official meeting on March 29, Jefferson, of course, was elected rector. Even before the new board had its first meeting, however, Jefferson convened the old board one last time in late February and pushed it to approve using the remaining funds to begin construction on more pavilions and dormitories.[163]

Although a crucial battle had been won on January 25 with the university's founding, victory was far from complete. An indication of the work yet to be done was conveyed by Jefferson in his response to Cabell's letter telling him of the favorable Senate vote. "I join with you in joy on the passage of the University bill," Jefferson happily wrote, and then quickly added: "But we shall fall miserably short in the execution of the large plan displayed to the world with the short funds proposed for its execution." Jefferson noted the buildings in progress and those yet to be constructed, the number of professorships to be filled, the scientific equipment and books that needed to be purchased, and he complained that the legislature had now authorized "the name of a University without the means of making it so." Jefferson then instructed Cabell to return to the legislature and lay claim on behalf of the university to any funds appropriated for but not yet used by counties in support of the pauper schools. Although Cabell in this instance countered that the time and mood were not right for this particular move, he assured Jefferson that he would return to the legislature to seek more funds after a respectable passage of time.[164]

In a very real sense, this exchange reflected the tone of the Jefferson-Cabell correspondence during the period of the university's construction. The next six years were marked by continuing struggles for more funds in order to enable Jefferson to complete his grand vision of building an institution unparalleled by any in the United States. With daily horseback rides down to the university grounds when health and weather permitted, and observation of the progress of construction through his telescope from Monticello at other times, Jefferson kept a close eye on his pet project, the "hobby" of his old age. And, never satisfied with the most recent appropriation, Jefferson constantly devised tactics and directed Cabell into the legislative fray to obtain more funds. Cabell, ever loyal, endeavored to carry out Jefferson's instructions although ill health, fatigue, and confessed embarrassment at times took their toll.[165]

Typical of Jefferson's frustrations with the pecuniary tightness of the

Virginia legislature was the wording of a letter he wrote to Cabell on January 22, 1820, a letter he suggested Cabell was at liberty to share with opponents as well as friends of the university. In it, Jefferson compared educational conditions in Virginia with those of a newer state that had been carved out of lands once considered part of the Old Dominion: "Kentucky, our daughter, planted since Virginia was a distinguished State, has an University [Transylvania], with fourteen professors and upwards of 200 students; while we, with a fund of a million and a half of dollars, ready raised and appropriated, are higgling without the heart to let it go to its use. If our Legislature does not heartily push our University, we must send our children for education to Kentucky or Cambridge. The latter will return them to us fanatics & Tories [and] the former will keep them to add to their population." Jefferson abhorred such a prospect, but declared that, if Virginia students had to go elsewhere for their education, "I would rather it should be to Kentucky than any other State, because she has more of the flavor of the old cask than any other." The important point to Jefferson, however, was his conviction that "all the States but our own are sensible that knowledge is power." In terms of the establishment of state universities Jefferson was largely correct. Beginning with Georgia in 1785 and North Carolina in 1789, a number of states had chartered state-supported universities years earlier, although none were as ambitious an undertaking as was the University of Virginia.[166]

Writing from Poplar Forest later in the same year, Jefferson complained that Virginia, once in the forefront of her sister colonies, was becoming "the Barbary of the Union." The little education available in the state, he wrote, "we import, like beggars, from other States, or import their beggars to bestow on us their miserable crumbs." Declaring that the contest for funds ought not be cast as one between the university and the public schools, he declared that there was sufficient money for both if only Virginia had an orderly system. "More money is now paid for the education of a part, than would be paid for that of the whole if systematically arranged," he contended.[167]

On the last day of 1821, the usually optimistic Jefferson admitted that the legislature's parsimony over the past year filled him "with gloom" and wrote to Cabell that "I perceive that I am not to live to see it [the University] opened."

Responding to an indication from Cabell that he was contemplating not standing for reelection when his current term in the Senate expired, Jefferson accused him of "desertion" and said that if anyone on the Board of Visitors had an excuse for withdrawing from service, it was he himself who no longer had "vigor of body nor mind left to keep the field." But, Jefferson admonished, "I will die in the last ditch. And so, I hope, will you, my friend, as well as our firm-breasted brothers and colleagues, Mr. Johnson and General Breckenridge," both of whom, like Cabell, were members of the legislature as well as visitors of the university. Cabell relented and moved forward with Johnson, Breckenridge, and other friends of the institution to try to obtain from the legislature a loan of $60,000, which Jefferson thought might be sufficient, on top of other funds already committed, to bring the university to completion. As would happen repeatedly, however, Jefferson's estimates fell short of the amount needed, especially after he determined to replicate at half-scale the Roman Pantheon as the library and centerpiece of the university. [168]

Jefferson strongly resisted the advice of those who suggested opening the university even before all the buildings were in place or the total faculty had been assembled, reasoning in a rather typical letter to Cabell: "Even with the whole funds, we shall be reduced to six professors, while Harvard will still prime it over us, with her twenty professors." In December of 1822, Jefferson reminded Cabell, who certainly needed no reminding, of their high aim for the institution in words that bear extensive quotation:

> The great object of our aim from the beginning, has been to make the establishment the most eminent in the United States, in order to draw to it the youth of every State, but especially of the south and west. We have proposed therefore, to call to it characters [professors] of the first order of science from Europe, as well as our own country; and, not only by the salaries and the comforts of their situation, but by the distinguished scale of its structure and preparation, and the promise of future eminence which these would hold up, to induce them to commit their reputation to its future fortunes. Had we built a barn for a college, and log huts for accommodations, should we ever have

had the assurance to propose to an European professor of that character to come to it? Why give up this important idea, when so near
its accomplishment that a single lift more effects it? ... To stop where
we are, is to abandon our high hopes, and become suitors to Yale and
Harvard for their secondary characters to become our first. Have we
been laboring then merely to get up another Hampden Sidney or
Lexington? Yet to this it sinks, if we abandon foreign aid [additional
funding]. The report of Rockfish Gap, sanctioned by the Legislature,
authorized us to aim at much higher things .... The opening of the
institution in a half-state of readiness would be the most fatal step
which could be adopted .... Taking our stand on commanding ground
at once will beckon every thing to it, and a reputation once established
will maintain itself for ages.[169]

Jefferson, having been deeply concerned about the divisive debates over the
restriction or extension of slavery into new states that resulted in the Missouri
Compromise of 1820, fretted that southern students in northern colleges were
being corrupted by "anti-Missourianism" and believed they would flock back to
Virginia if only the university could be brought to maturity. If his views were
nationalistic during his presidency, in his declining years Jefferson adhered more
and more rigidly to states' rights doctrine and, with the Missouri question sounding a "firebell in the night," feared for the survival of the Union and the future of
Virginia. He saw his unfinished university as essential to the preservation of *his*
views of the fundamental precepts of republicanism even while proclaiming it as
an institution totally unfettered by restrictive doctrines, political or religious.[170]

National politics aside, Jefferson's fixed attention on pushing for the completion of the university consumed much of his attention and at the same time took
a severe toll emotionally as well as physically on Joseph Cabell. When Cabell had
informed Jefferson in February 1821 that a bill permitting a loan to the university
had finally passed, he pleaded with Jefferson that "It is the anxious wish of our
best friends, and of no one more than myself, that the money now granted may be
sufficient to finish the buildings. We must not come here again on that subject."

Noting mounting animosity toward the rising costs of the university project, he further informed Jefferson several weeks later: "The popular cry [in the legislature] is that there is too much finery and too much extravagance."[171]

There can be little question that, in comparison to other collegiate institutions of the day, the University of Virginia was indeed an expensive venture. Jefferson's estimates of expenses continually fell short of the mark. Not only did the visitors appeal to the legislature for additional help, they also borrowed from banks and from the Literary Fund and employed a collector to go after delinquent subscriptions. Eventually the legislature was persuaded to suspend interest on the first loan, grant another, and finally even to cancel the principal on both loans. When a final tally was disclosed in 1828, it was revealed that, up to that year, total expenditures for the pavilions and dormitories totaled $236,678 while the Rotunda had been built for $57,749. (Jefferson had estimated the Rotunda's cost at $46,847.) In 1830, the entire property belonging to the university was valued at $333,095.[172]

Mr. Jefferson's University had in the end required a great deal more than the annual appropriation of $15,000 provided for in Senator Joseph Cabell's 1817 rider to a pauper school bill. Perhaps one might be forgiven for suggesting, however, that the state of Virginia got a bargain in the deal.

Chapter Ten

JEFFERSON'S EDUCATIONAL LEGACY

This institution will be based on the illimitable freedom of the human mind. For here we are not afraid to follow truth wherever it may lead, nor tolerate any error so long as reason is left free to combat it.

— Thomas Jefferson to William Roscoe,
December 27, 1820[173]

When the first students began to enroll at the University of Virginia on March 7, 1825, they became the initial beneficiaries of Thomas Jefferson's educational legacy. That legacy, however, included far more than a stately group of classical buildings neatly arranged around an open space soon to be covered with grass and lined with trees. Jefferson's legacy was framed by a philosophy of education that was reflected in much more than the buildings and layout of his "academical village." It further encompassed his views regarding the broad range of advanced studies, mode of organization and governance, qualifications and expectations of faculty and students, and secular orientation of his university. Perhaps most significantly, the Jeffersonian legacy incorporated larger social and political purposes to which he pledged the university *and* the elementary and secondary institutions that were always a vital component of his conception of a complete system of education.

As noted when describing earlier phases of Jefferson's evolving educational plans, specific details changed over time. He made both academic and architectural adjustments as useful advice, advancing knowledge, altered circumstances, and his assessment of economic and political realities of the moment dictated. Jefferson was entirely consistent, however, in defining the broad outlines of his plans and purpose. To Jefferson, education should equip *all* citizens of the new nation with the skills and sensibilities that would enable each to become self-sufficient, able to pursue happiness, and capable of maintaining a republican society. From the outset, Jefferson's vision for education in Virginia included an entire system, not only erudition for a leadership class. It is significant in this regard to note that in composing the Rockfish Gap Report, Jefferson took into consideration not only the direct charge to the commission of determining the site for the university, but stressed again that a solid precollegiate system was essential for the creation and advancement of an educated republican citizenry. In that report he specified the objectives of the "primary" or basic levels of education as follows:

- To give every citizen the information he needs for the transaction of his own business;
- To enable him to calculate for himself, and to express and preserve his ideas, his contracts and accounts, in writing;
- To improve, by reading, his morals and faculties;
- To understand his duties to his neighbors and country, and to discharge with competence the functions confided to him by either;
- To know his rights; to exercise with order and justice those he retains; and to choose with discretion the fiduciary of those he delegates; and to notice their conduct with diligence, with candor, and judgment;
- And, in general, to observe with intelligence and faithfulness all the social relations under which he shall be placed.[174]

Neither the passage of time, scores of blue ribbon commissions since Jefferson's day, nor the pronouncements of a growing line of claimants to the title of "the education president" have resulted in a better set of goals for the instruction of the public at large. Surely Jefferson's title as "the first" education president is uncontested in terms of both time and substance, even though it was not until many decades after his death—indeed, after the Civil War—that Virginia put into place a statewide system of universal elementary education.

So strongly did Jefferson feel about the relationship between literacy and citizenship that he once considered denying the privileges of citizenship to those who were illiterate. While urging the passage of his revised education bill in 1817, Jefferson not only stressed the duty of the state to provide for the education of all of its citizens, but reflected as well on the reciprocal obligations that citizens had to the state. Although reluctant to have the state make attendance compulsory, he did insert a provision in this new bill stating that "no person unborn or under the age of twelve years at the passing of this act, and who is compos mentis, shall, after the age of fifteen years, be a citizen of this commonwealth until he or she can read readily in some tongue, native or acquired." While recognizing that it might be better to "tolerate the rare instance of a parent refusing to let his child be educated" than to force a child to attend school against the wishes of a parent, Jefferson's reasoning was clear: "If we do not force instruction, let us at least strengthen the motive to receive it when offered." As it happened, Jefferson need not have agonized over this issue, for Cabell prudently struck this provision and others likely to distract from the chief purpose of the education bill before submitting it to the legislature. Even so, the bill met with defeat.[175]

Jefferson's view of the public "pursuit of happiness" as well as the private benefits of education underlay his advocacy of libraries and a free press as well as a system of publicly supported schools. "The basis of our government being the opinion of the people, the very first object should be to keep that right; and were it left to me to decide whether we should have a government without newspapers, or newspapers without a government, I should not hesitate a moment to prefer the latter," wrote Jefferson in 1787. He hastened to add, however: "But I should mean that every man should receive those papers and be capable of reading them." Jefferson's aphorism points yet again to his fundamental belief that in a free society, "the people are the only censors of their governors" and the best guardians of their own liberties.[176]

Jefferson's advocacy of public support for the education of the mass of the population was in many ways an exception to his general premise that government should interfere as little as possible with the natural functioning of society. As historian Peter Onuf observed, "Spending on education constituted the grand

and significant exception to Jefferson's minimal state, for this was precisely the kind of public investment that would foster the welfare of the rising generation without wasting its future prospects." Jefferson stated the matter directly in a letter to Madison: "I am not a friend to a very energetic government. It is always oppressive." Yet in an expanded version of the same letter sent to another correspondent, Jefferson stated that providing the public with access to information "is the most certain, and the most legitimate engine of government. Educate and inform the whole mass of the people," he continued. "Enable them to see that it is [in] their interest to preserve peace and order, and they will preserve it. [And] it requires no very high degree of education to convince them of this. They are the only sure reliance for the preservation of our liberty."[177]

In the same report in which Jefferson spelled out the aims of education for the general population, he was no less specific when it came to defining the educational purposes for those who would be recipients of more advanced education and thus would likely be called into service as governors of the citizenry. Here again his list of objectives for university education bears quoting:

- To form the statesmen, legislators and judges, on whom public prosperity and individual happiness are so much to depend;
- To expound the principles and structure of government, the laws which regulate the intercourse of nations, those formed municipally for our own government, and a sound spirit of legislation, which, banishing all arbitrary and unnecessary restraint on individual action, shall leave us free to do whatever does not violate the equal rights of another;
- To harmonize and promote the interests of agriculture, manufactures and commerce, and by well informed views of political economy to give a free scope to the public industry;
- To develop the reasoning faculties of our youth, enlarge their minds, cultivate their morals, and instill into them the precepts of virtue and order;
- To enlighten them with mathematical and physical sciences,

which advance the arts, and administer to the health, the subsistence, and comforts of human life;

- And, generally to form them to habits of reflection and correct action, rendering them examples of virtue to others, and of happiness within themselves.[178]

These were the goals set for what Jefferson at times called "the natural aristocracy ... [of] virtue and talents" or "the most precious gifts of nature"—those individuals drawn from every rank in society who should compose the professional class from which some would be drawn and entrusted with the highest offices and responsibilities in the society. Although Jefferson firmly believed that everyone was endowed with a shared moral sense and that a plowman could determine right from wrong as easily or perhaps even better than a professor, he also held that offices of public trust should go to those who had pursued learning to the highest levels. It was on this very point that Jeffersonian Democrats differed so markedly from their successors, the Jacksonian Democrats.[179]

The features that Jefferson put in place at the University of Virginia to bring these goals within reach gave a distinctive character to the institution that notably separated it from other seats of higher learning of the day. The University of Virginia was a maverick institution. It established a new pattern for American higher education, albeit one that was only slowly incorporated into the nation's leading universities.

Among the significant departures from tradition that marked the university's opening was Jefferson's insistence that the professors recruited be "of the first order of science" in their academic fields. The prevailing faculty pattern at most colleges and universities was characterized by hiring a few classically trained generalists, often assisted by young tutors, to lead students through a set of standard texts employing a recitation format. Jefferson wanted professors who, as experts in specific fields of knowledge, would lecture on subjects that, in his familiar words, were "useful to us at this day, and in their *highest* degree." He was aiming to create a university much more akin to modern graduate and professional schools than to the more limited collegiate institutions of the day. It is for this reason that the university did not offer bachelor's degrees until long after Jefferson's death. The diplomas he and the initial Board of Visitors authorized were of two grades, "the highest of doctor, the second of graduate."[180]

As early as 1800 Jefferson had suggested to Joseph Priestley that the university he was contemplating would probably have to turn to Europe at the outset for professors of the highest standing, but when he began to cast about for professors for Central College, he first looked to Americans. In addition to Samuel Knox and Thomas Cooper, in 1818 Jefferson extended an offer to Nathaniel Bowditch, whose mathematical and navigational acclaim had earlier prompted invitations from Harvard and West Point, both of which he had declined. Likewise, Jefferson's projected offer of $2,000 and a rent-free pavilion with a garden also failed to draw him southward from Massachusetts, where his income as president of Essex Fire and Marine Insurance Company was considerably higher than Jefferson could offer. Jefferson then turned to Harvard linguist George Ticknor, with whom he had enjoyed a steady correspondence for several years. While studying at the University of Göttingen, Ticknor had extolled the academic freedom and the stimulating climate of scholarship that professors in Germany experienced, points that were not lost on Jefferson as he contemplated his own university's features. However, neither Jefferson's description of his university plans nor the enticements of Virginia's "genial climate" could entice Ticknor to abandon Cambridge for Charlottesville.[181]

When these overtures failed, Jefferson became all the more convinced that he would have to turn to Europe to find academics of the highest caliber. As the buildings around the Lawn were nearing completion in the spring of 1824, the Board of Visitors went on record as agreeing with Jefferson in the opinion that "to obtain professors of the first order of science in their respective lines, they must resort principally to Europe." On behalf of the board, Jefferson enlisted Francis Walker Gilmer, a young Charlottesville lawyer and son of an esteemed Jefferson friend, to undertake the mission of going abroad in search of professorial talent. Recognizing that European scholars of the absolute top rank would hardly be inclined to give up their posts to come to an as-yet unfinished university, Jefferson reasoned that Gilmer should aim to recruit the top scholars' protégés, young men

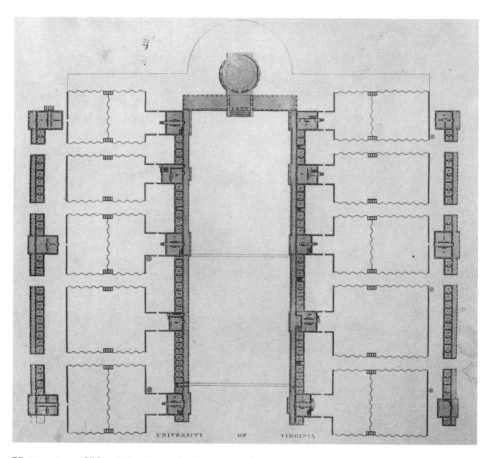

University of Virginia *(second edition, 1825) engraved by Peter Maverick. (Courtesy Special Collections, University of Virginia)*

who, as the historian Phillip Bruce phrased it, might be "treading impatiently on the heels of the veterans." Jefferson paved the way for Gilmer by giving him a letter of introduction to, among others, Richard Rush, the American minister in London. Jefferson explained Gilmer's mission to Rush and asked for the ambassador's assistance in making contacts with Great Britain's leading scholars. Universities in England, Scotland, and Ireland were deemed logical recruiting grounds in that scholars there would share with Americans a "common language, habits, and customs"—or at least Jefferson hoped that would be the case.[182]

It is somewhat ironic that the first scholar to sign a contract with Gilmer was George Blaettermann, a German by birth and education who was then living in London. Blaettermann had corresponded with Jefferson regarding an appoint-

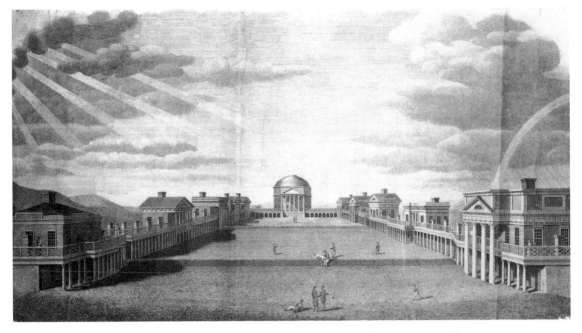

University of Virginia *(from an 1824 drawing) engraved by Benjamin Tanner.*
(Courtesy Special Collections, University of Virginia)

ment in 1823 and had been recommended to Jefferson by Ticknor. Gilmer met with
Blaettermann in London and offered him a contract as professor of modern languages at a salary of $1,000 plus a tuition fee of $50 for every pupil who pursued his
courses only, $30 for those who would attend another professor's lectures, and $25
from each student who would attend two other "schools," or professors. Whether
because of Blaettermann's strong accent or other reasons, Gilman's decision to
offer this German scholar a base salary of $1,000 plus student fees was less than
the maximum of $1,500 plus fees that had been authorized and would be offered
other professors he recruited. Nonetheless, the range of languages Blaettermann
agreed to teach was impressive: French, Spanish, Italian, German, and Anglo-
Saxon, along with the history and geography of each country. Blaettermann also
announced that, if students were interested, he was prepared to give lessons in the
vernacular languages of Denmark, Sweden, Holland, and Portugal![183]

Gilmer faced difficulties in trying to persuade some other promising scholars of the advantages to be had in casting their lot with the novel American
university being built in a decidedly non-cosmopolitan part of Virginia. He was

disappointed in not finding anyone at the University of Edinburgh willing to transplant himself to Virginia, but finally was able to accomplish his mission by signing five foreign professors. In addition to Blaettermann, Gilmer received an enthusiastic acceptance from Thomas Key, a graduate of Trinity College who had studied medicine at Guy's Hospital in London and had just received a master's degree from Cambridge University. As mathematics professor, Key was expected to teach algebra, trigonometry, plane and spherical geometry, mensuration, navigation, conic sections, differential calculus, and military and civil architecture. He was joined by a classicist from the same university, George Long, who was recruited as the professor of ancient languages. The 1824 curriculum set by the board specified that the "higher grade" of Latin and Greek would be Long's responsibility, along with Hebrew, rhetoric, belles-lettres, and ancient history and geography. Charles Bonnycastle, who had been educated by his father, a noted mathematician at the Royal Military Academy, became the professor of natural philosophy. Included in his domain were mechanics, statics, hydrostatics, hydraulics, pneumatics, acoustics, optics, and astronomy. Dr. Robley Dunglison became professor of anatomy and medicine, specialties that included surgery, the history of medicine, physiology, pathology, material medica, and pharmacy. Dunglison, a Scot, had obtained medical degrees in London and Germany and had a diploma from the Society of Apothecaries.

These appointments were soon augmented by the addition of two Americans, both of whom had become naturalized citizens: John Patton Emmet, who had been born in Ireland, became the professor of natural history, and George Tucker, a native of Bermuda, was appointed professor of moral philosophy. Emmet had attended West Point and had earned a medical degree from the College of Physicians and Surgeons in New York. His assignment included botany, zoology, mineralogy, chemistry, geology, and rural economy. Tucker was a graduate of the College of William and Mary, a noted author, and congressman. His teaching duties included "mental science generally, including ideology, general grammar, logic and ethics."[184]

The visitors had a more difficult time identifying the person to fill the final vacancy, the professorship of law. Above all others, this was the position that Jefferson considered it vital for an American to occupy. The post was first offered to George Gilmer, who, after considerable thought, declined. William Wirt, attorney general of the United States from 1817–1829 and the chief prosecutor in the conspiracy trial against Aaron Burr, was another candidate. The board, against Jefferson's wishes, so wanted Wirt that he was offered the presidency of the university along with the law professorship, but he declined both appointments. Thereafter the board agreed to abide by Jefferson's wish that the university be governed by the visitors and the faculty as a whole under a rotating chairmanship, and that there not be a chief executive officer other than the rector—a system that prevailed until 1904. Not until July 1826, a full year after classes had begun in the other schools, did the board finally secure the services of John T. Lomax, a Fredericksburg attorney who satisfied all the requirements deemed necessary for the position. His nativity and his political views were in accord with the wishes of Jefferson and the Board of Visitors.[185]

The qualifications set for professors included more than the potential for eminence in their respective areas of learning. When it was once suggested by Cabell that Jefferson consider an attorney who was a relative for the law professorship, Jefferson replied: "The individual named in your letter is one of the best, and to me the dearest of living men." But Jefferson reminded Cabell that they had, "from the beginning, considered the high qualification of our professors as the only means by which we could give to our institution splendor and pre-eminence over all its sister seminaries." Jefferson then set forth the primary dictum that was to guide the visitors in making appointments: "The only question, therefore, we can ever ask ourselves, as to any candidate, will be, is he the most highly qualified?" Jefferson then pointed to other considerations as well, noting that "a man is not qualified for a professor, knowing nothing but merely his own profession. He should be otherwise well educated as to the sciences generally; able to converse understandingly with the scientific men with whom he is associated, and to assist in the councils of the Faculty on any subject of science on which they may have occasion to deliberate." Jefferson further made it clear in framing the governance of the university that professors were expected to be fully committed to their teaching and studies and thus "shall engage in no other pursuits of emolument unconnected with the service of the University without the consent of the Visitors."[186]

Perhaps the most striking feature of the Jeffersonian educational legacy was his dedication of the University of Virginia to the principles of intellectual freedom. At a time when conformity to doctrinal positions of sponsoring denominations was still expected on the part of faculty in both English and American institutions of higher learning, Jefferson launched his university with the promise that scholars at Virginia could enjoy the "illimitable freedom of the human mind." In recruiting professors, Jefferson assured candidates that, given the liberal character and tolerant disposition of members of the board, they would in effect have lifetime tenure in their posts and would be unfettered in their teaching. Unlike institutions at which the board of trustees determined books that might be used in various classes, the Virginia trustees concurred with Jefferson that the choice of texts should be left with the individual professors since they would be much more knowledgeable about their respective fields than would any member of the board.[187]

This is not to say that there was not a disconnect between Jefferson's professed high *ideals* and his own conception of practical restraints regarding free expression at his university, however. While he could in good conscience proclaim that "I have sworn upon the altar of God eternal hostility against every form of tyranny over the mind of man" with respect to religious bigotry, he was decidedly more cautious when it came to political persuasions and sectional controversies, especially in his latter years. On matters related to government, his institution was in actuality to be dedicated to the principles of Republicanism as Jefferson understood those principles. Madison agreed with Jefferson that the best safeguard against the intrusion of heretical political theories was the selection of "an able and orthodox professor" in the fields they considered most critical to the continuance of the principles of 1776, law and government. Before the visitors appointed a professor for the school of law (in which government would also be taught), therefore, special conditions were placed on the person who would hold that office. Not only should the professor be an American, but he should insure that his students were well acquainted with democratic-republican scripture. Thus, while all other professors at the university were given total freedom in the selection of books to be used in their courses, an exception was made in the case of the professor of law. Jefferson and Madison, with the consent of the board, believed that on the matter of law and government, they were in fact likely to be more knowledgeable than some as-yet unidentified professor. Accordingly, they determined that the visitors should identify certain texts that should form the basis of the curriculum in law and government. The texts included the Declaration of Independence, John Locke's *Treatises on Government*, Algernon Sidney's *Discourses On Government*, *The Federalist Papers*, and Madison's Virginia Report of 1799 on the Alien and Sedition Laws. Madison suggested that George Washington's first inaugural and farewell addresses be added to the list, a suggestion that Jefferson heartedly endorsed. Madison also cautioned that the prescribed texts should be viewed as a guide or a standard "without requiring an unqualified conformity to them, which indeed might not in every instance be possible." The board approved the list at its meeting on March 4, 1825.[188]

That Jefferson was somewhat uncomfortable in specifying any texts was evidenced in the fact that he cautioned Cabell several weeks before the board meeting to hold the pending resolution in confidence, for "the less such things are spoken of before hand, the less obstruction is contrived to be thrown in their way." It is important to emphasize, however, that the list adopted by the Board of Visitors for study in the school of law was *pre*scriptive, not *pro*scriptive in nature. Adoption of these fundamental treatises did not preclude the use of other texts. The intent was to insure that the students received grounding in the "correct" principles of American government. Dumas Malone commented in this regard that complete consistency cannot be rightly claimed for Jefferson, but that "it is safe to say that no other American of his generation did more to remove shackles from the mind." Malone observed further: "And, judged by contemporary standards, the institution he had planned was to be one of notable liberality."[189]

Although the term was not then in vogue, the academic freedom Jefferson thought important for professors applied to the university's students as well. A basic ingredient in student freedom was total election of studies. Jefferson informed Ticknor of his intentions in this regard by writing, "I am not fully informed of the practices at Harvard, but there is one from which we shall certainly vary, although it has been copied, I believe, by nearly every college and academy in the United States. That is, the holding the students all to one prescribed course of reading, and disallowing exclusive application to those branches only which are to qualify them for the particular vocations to which they are destined. We shall, on the contrary, allow them uncontrolled choice in the lectures they shall choose to attend, and requiring elementary qualification only, and sufficient age." Accordingly, in regulations adopted on October 4, 1824, the visitors specified that "Every student shall be free to attend the schools of his choice, and no other than he chooses."[190]

The elective system, today a feature of almost every college and university in the land, spread only slowly and in limited degrees to other colleges before the Civil War. Ticknor pressed for changes at Harvard, but not until the administration of Charles W. Eliot (1869-1909) did Harvard energetically adopt an elective format. Although typically given credit as being the father of the elective system, Eliot recognized Jefferson as the one who first implemented and "preach[ed] with the utmost persistence the underlying doctrine of the elective system." He wanted every student, said Eliot, "to follow the line of his inclination in the selection of his course of study."[191]

In yet another respect students at Virginia were given liberties that were denied at other higher education institutions of the day. Compulsory chapel attendance, a bedrock requirement elsewhere, received no sanction at Virginia. Jefferson suggested that students and faculty might hold worship services in a room in the Rotunda, but construction of a separate chapel he deemed unnecessary and potentially a source of sectarian friction. Here again other institutions did not follow the university's lead in terms of voluntary worship until after the Civil War and, at many denominationally sponsored institutions, chapel attendance remained compulsory until deep into the twentieth century.

Jefferson's insistence that students be free to worship (or not) as they pleased merely added fuel to the fire for those who opposed the secular—or "Godless"—orientation of Mr. Jefferson's University. While Jefferson had made provision for a professor of theology in his 1814 curricular proposal sent to Peter Carr and the Central College trustees, he later followed the suggestion of Thomas Cooper when devising plans for the University of Virginia and dropped that chair from his proposed professorships (as he had done earlier as governor when attempting to reform William and Mary). Jefferson emphasized, however, that religion would be taught as a natural component of courses in Hebrew, Greek, and Latin and in the study of history that would accompany instruction in those languages. Moreover, studies in moral philosophy and ethics that developed "those moral obligations in which all sects agree" would be, he stated in an 1822 annual report, both constitutionally and academically appropriate.[192]

On behalf of the board, Jefferson labored to stem the tide of public opinion that saw in this latitudinarian approach a hostility toward religion. In the 1822 report he insisted that "the relations which exist between man and his Maker, and the duties resulting from those relations, are the most interesting and important to every human being, and the most incumbent on his study and investigation." To have no instruction in religion would create "a chasm" at the university, he stated. Incorporating an idea that Samuel Knox had outlined in his essay presented to the American Philosophical Society in the mid-1790s (see chapter 4), Jefferson proposed that each religious sect establish seminaries adjacent to the university. This, he said, would give the seminarians "ready and convenient access" to studies at the university and at the same time would enable students at the university to attend worship services with others of their own particular denomination. "Such an arrangement," Jefferson wrote, "would complete the circle of useful sciences embraced by this institution, and would fill the chasm now existing on principles which would leave inviolate the constitutional freedom of religion, the most unalienable and sacred of all human rights."[193]

Jefferson claimed to be a Christian "in the only sense in which he [Jesus] wished any one to be; sincerely attached to his doctrines, in preference to all others," yet his denial of the divinity of Jesus Christ and his lifelong criticism of narrow-minded ministers and "corruptions of Christianity" made him an inviting target for adherents to doctrinal orthodoxy. Moreover, his failure to provide for a professor of divinity, his rejection of compulsory chapel, and his earlier move to hire the free-thinking Thomas Cooper as one of the first faculty members of Central College combined to arouse considerable controversy and opposition. Jefferson refused to back away from his support of Cooper and persuaded a reluctant board of the newly chartered University of Virginia that it should respect the earlier offer made to him. John Holt Rice, both a Presbyterian minister and an early supporter of the university, led a campaign against Cooper. This placed the institution in an embarrassing situation until Cooper, aware of the resentment against him, removed himself from candidacy in 1820. Jefferson branded Presbyterian clergymen as the loudest and "most intolerant of all" sectarian leaders and asserted that they opposed the university because "they wish to see no instruction of which they have not the exclusive direction." But Presbyterians were not alone in questioning Jefferson's beliefs and decisions with respect to religion—and Cooper—at the university. Madison did not agree with Jefferson regarding Cooper's appointment, nor did fellow visitors John Hartwell Cocke, Chapman Johnson, and Joseph Cabell. As Cocke put the dilemma, "I think our old friend went a little too far ... [but] we must stand around him ... and extricate him as well as we can." It is understandable then that his invitation to the leading denominations to erect seminaries near (but not on) the university grounds naturally was suspect in the minds of many. To religious critics of the university, the institution deserved the "Godless" reputation being imputed to it. This charge of infidelity was only somewhat softened under Madison's rectorship several years later when the faculty began inviting ministers to hold Sunday services in the Rotunda.[194]

There was yet another aspect of Jefferson's university that was unusual—and for a time, at least—unworkable. Jefferson's belief in freedom caused him to steer a liberal course when it came to student discipline. He was fully aware of the problems associated with a large body of young men brought together over an extended period of time. He confessed anxieties in this regard to Cooper after the latter had become a professor and then president of the University of South Carolina. Upon hearing of some student disturbances at South Carolina, Jefferson wrote, "The article of discipline is the most difficult in American education. Premature ideas of independence, too little repressed by parents, beget a spirit of insubordination, which is the great obstacle to science with us, and a principle cause of its decay since the revolution. I look to it with dismay at our institution, as a breaker ahead, which I am far from being confident we shall be able to weather."[195]

Although concerned, Jefferson determined to institute a system of student government that would encourage students to assume responsibility for their conduct. "Pride of character, laudable ambition, and moral dispositions are innate correctives of the indiscretions of that lively age," he had explained in the Rockfish Gap Report. Believing that "the affectionate deportment between father and son offers in truth the best example for that of tutor and pupil," Jefferson's plans called for a student-run Board of Censors to act as the principal judicial body. Professor Robley Dunglison called Jefferson's scheme for student self-government a "fanciful" idea, but the faculty had no choice but to abide by the founder's wishes.[196]

Although some years later this progressive concept evolved into a student-run honor system at the University of Virginia, Jefferson found to his great disappointment that at least some of the students in Charlottesville were not prepared by temperament or prior education to accept the academic demands and associated freedom of the university. A few "vicious irregularities" during the early months of the university's existence climaxed with the first of a succession of major disturbances by the fall. After the first riot, Jefferson assembled the students, faculty, and visitors in the Rotunda and began to admonish the students for their misconduct. Choked with emotion and unable to go on, the eighty-two-year-old Jefferson yielded the floor to Visitor Chapman Johnson, who rebuked the students and asked for the leaders of the disturbance to confess their guilt. Fourteen stepped forward in admission of the part they had played in the riotous behavior, one of whom was one of Jefferson's grandnephews. Upon seeing a member of his own family admit guilt, Jefferson could not disguise his grief. With the collapse of Jefferson's plan for student self-government crumbled also one of his most cherished convictions. Disillusioned, he encouraged the Board of Visitors to appeal to the General Assembly for authority to tighten regulations within the university. In the years that followed Jefferson's death, the faculty and visitors multiplied the rules as the students multiplied their offenses. The tide began to turn back towards Jefferson's idealistic vision of student self-government when, in 1842, two years after the murder of a popular professor by a drunken student, Virginia students adopted an "Honor Code" which contained the essence of Jefferson's belief in individual integrity and self-discipline. It remains as one of the most distinctive and significant features of the university—and a point of continuing tension.[197]

To give a full account of Jefferson's educational legacy, we must also acknowledge that while his educational plans proved to be bolder and more progressive than many of his contemporaries could appreciate, he was less bold and progressive than we today might wish, limited by his own and his society's assumptions. This is true in varying degrees with respect to his opinions on the education of women, African Americans, and Native Americans.

Although Jefferson's plan of 1779 and later renditions called for the education of girls through the elementary grades, he did not envision *public* support for the education of women beyond that point. He did, however, favor the continuing education of women within the family circle for reasons of both utility and ornamentality. Reflecting the accepted definition of the "woman's sphere" in the early American social order, Jefferson reasoned that, as future wives and mothers, young women needed instruction in household economy as well as in other realms. Jefferson's letters to his two daughters who survived childhood and to his granddaughters stressed the importance of learning French, Spanish, and Latin, as well as gaining proficiency in their own language. While living in Paris, he enrolled his daughters in the Abbaye Royale de Panthemont, a convent school considered the most genteel in Paris. Throughout their youth, he encouraged them in the fine arts, recommended books, established rigid schedules for their studies, and filled his letters with advice on manners and morals. He pointed to the lasting value of education for women, as it was for men, in a letter to his daughter Martha in 1787: "The object most interesting to me for the residue of my life, will be to see you both [daughters Martha and Maria] developing daily those principles of virtue and goodness which will make you valuable to others and happy in your selves, and acquiring those talents and that degree of science which will guard you at all times against ennui, the most dangerous poison of life. A mind employed is always happy. This is the true secret, the grand recipe for felicity."[198]

While Jefferson saw the education of women, however circumscribed, as an activity to be encouraged, he was far less open-minded in his opinions about the education of black slaves. While his sweeping scheme for publicly supported education was closed to African Americans and he seems to have made no efforts to provide private opportunities for his own slaves, several slaves at Monticello and Poplar Forest did learn to read and write. Surviving letters and accounts written to and by Jefferson's slaves indicate a fair degree of functional literacy and numeracy, at least among some domestic servants and those in skilled crafts. On a larger scale, a surviving fragment of a letter to Quaker activist Robert Pleasants suggests that Jefferson *may* have been at least willing to entertain the notion of educating slaves. Considering Pleasants's plan for the education for slaves, Jefferson somewhat passively replied that his own plan for publicly supported education could perhaps be modified to include black children. Practically speaking, however, Jefferson seems to have taken no active role, privately or publicly, in advancing opportunities for furthering formal education among enslaved or free blacks—except for purposes of their return to Africa.[199]

A conviction that "deep seated prejudices" held by whites, "ten thousand recollections" of abuse on the part of blacks, and "the real distinctions that nature has made" foreclosed in Jefferson's mind the possibility of the two races ever living in harmony. When working on the revisal of Virginia laws in the late 1770s, Jefferson prepared for the Virginia legislature a plan for the gradual emancipation of slaves. He proposed as an amendment to a bill defining the status of slaves that all children of slaves born after a certain date be offered training at public expense in farming, the arts and sciences, or other fields according to their abilities. Upon arriving at adulthood, women at eighteen and men at twenty-one, these descendants of slaves were to be provided with arms, tools, household implements, and domestic animals and then colonized in Africa as "a free and independent people" in alliance with and initially under the protection of the United States. To replace the expatriated slaves, Jefferson recommended the importation of white indentured servants from Europe. Jefferson's plan was neither adopted by the Virginia legislature nor acted upon by Jefferson himself.[200]

Jefferson was less ambivalent about the equality of Native Americans with whites: he considered Native Americans to be equal in intelligence, physical strength, and moral sense to *Homo sapiens Europeaneus*—in essence, they were white people who wore moccasins and breechcloths. With respect to the education of Native Americans, Jefferson preferred that the federal government rather than religious denominations or private societies "civilize" them. Good deist as he was, he feared the influence of Christian missionaries among the Native Americans and compared the evangelists to tribal medicine men—enemies of progress, bent upon keeping Indians in ignorance. As with his reform of the Indian School at William and Mary, Jefferson wanted individuals with the sensitivities and respect of anthropologists to take the lead in dealings with the American aborigines.[201]

Any summary of Thomas Jefferson's educational legacy must thus take into account the context of the times *and* the negative as well as positive judgments that might be made by those of our own and succeeding generations. While Jefferson was in some ways a product of his time, he was most significantly the prophet of later times. His labors on behalf of the education of citizens showed him to be far in advance of the thinking of his day. His lack of sustained attention to the education of those who, in his time and place, were outside the realm of citizenship is understandable even though lamentable.

Jefferson died on July 4, 1826, justly proud of his achievement as the Father of the University of Virginia, a university that he set on a distinctive course far in advance of other institutions of higher education. If his struggle for over four decades on behalf of publicly funded elementary and secondary schools might be reckoned a failure, it was a failure embedded in the limited vision of those whose religious, social, and political views thwarted his numerous attempts to bring such a system into existence. His plans were not perfect, nor his judgment always unclouded, realities that Jefferson certainly understood. Yet, whatever his personal or philosophical shortcomings as judged by later standards, Jefferson's insistence for nearly half a century on the necessity and justness of public support for the education of all citizens places us in his debt. It may well be, as Dumas Malone once observed, that had Jefferson's educational plan of 1779 (or its later iterations) been enacted and proven effective in practice, "it probably would have been listed with the statute for religious freedom among his greatest achievements."[202]

In the final analysis, perhaps Jefferson's most enduring legacy is the dictum that the current generation must chart its own course in matters educational as in other ways. He warned against ascribing to men of the previous ages a superhuman wisdom. As successive generations endeavor to adjust their educational goals and structures to the demands of their time, his advice penned in an 1816 letter seems appropriate to bear in mind: "Laws and institutions must go hand in hand with the progress of the human mind. As that becomes more developed, more enlightened, as new discoveries are made, new truths disclosed, and manners and opinions change with the change of circumstances, institutions must advance also, and keep pace with the times. We might as well require a man to wear still the coat which fitted him as a boy, as [for] civilized society to remain ever under the regimen of their barbarous ancestors."[203]

ABBREVIATIONS

Adams   Herbert B. Adams, *Thomas Jefferson and the University of Virginia.* Washington, D.C.: Government Printing Office, 1888.

APS   American Philosophical Society

Barringer   Paul Brandon Barringer, *University of Virginia: Its History, Influence, Equipment and Characteristics.* 2 vols. New York: Lewis Publishing Co., 1904.

Bruce   Philip Alexander Bruce, *History of the University of Virginia, 1819-1919,* 5 vols. New York: The Macmillan Co., 1920-1922.

Cappon   *The Adams-Jefferson Letters: The Complete Correspondence between Thomas Jefferson and Abigail and John Adams.* Lester J. Cappon, ed. 2 vols. Chapel Hill: University of North Carolina Press, 1959.

Honeywell   Roy J. Honeywell, *The Educational Work of Thomas Jefferson.* Cambridge: Harvard University Press, 1931.

K& P   *The Life and Selected Writings of Thomas Jefferson.* Adrienne Koch and William Peden, eds. New York: The Modern Library, 1972.

LC   Library of Congress

Letters   *Early History of the University of Virginia as Contained in the Letters of Thomas Jefferson and Joseph C. Cabell.* Nathaniel F. Cabell, ed. Richmond, VA: J. W. Randolph, 1856.

L&B   *The Writings of Thomas Jefferson.* Andrew A. Lipscomb and Albert Ellery Bergh, eds. Washington, D.C.: Thomas Jefferson Memorial Association, 1903.

Malone   Malone, Dumas, *Jefferson and His Time*, 6 vols. Boston: Little, Brown and Co., 1948.

Notes   Thomas Jefferson, *Notes on the State of Virginia,* William Peden, ed. Chapel Hill: University of North Carolina Press, [1787], 1950.

Papers   *The Papers of Thomas Jefferson*, Julian P. Boyd, ed., et al. Princeton, NJ: Princeton University Press, 1950 -.

Shawen   Neil McDowell Shawen, "The Casting of a Lengthened Shadow: Thomas Jefferson's Role in Determining the Site for a State University in Virginia." Ed.D. diss., George Washington University, 1980.

Smith   *The Republic of Letters: The Correspondence between Thomas Jefferson and James Madison, 1776-1826.* James Morton Smith, ed. 3 vols. New York: W. W. Norton & Company, 1995.

TJ   Thomas Jefferson as the writer or recipient of correspondence

U.Va.   Special Collections, Alderman Library, University of Virginia

VMHB   *The Virginia Magazine of History and Biography*

Works   *The Works of Thomas Jefferson.* Paul Leicester Ford, ed. New York: G. P. Putnam's Sons, 1905.

Writings   Peterson, Merrill D., *Thomas Jefferson Writings.* New York: The Library of America, 1984.

In most instances, irregular spelling and punctuation have been modernized where appropriate in quoted material.

NOTES

1   TJ to Abbé José Correia da Serra, October 24, 1820, Thomas Jefferson Papers, Library of Congress (hereafter LC) and Paul Leicester Ford, ed., *The Works of Thomas Jefferson* (New York: G. P. Putnam's Sons, 1905) 12:166-69 (hereafter *Works*); TJ to Joseph C. Cabell, January 13, 1823, in Nathaniel F. Cabell, ed., *Early History of the University of Virginia as Contained in the Letters of Thomas Jefferson and Joseph C. Cabell* (Richmond, VA: J. W. Randolph, 1856), 267-68 (hereafter *Letters*); TJ to Cabell, January 14, 1818, *Letters*, 106.

2   TJ to Charles Yancey, January 6, 1816, LC; TJ to Richard Price, January 8, 1789, in Julian P. Boyd, et al., eds., *The Papers of Thomas Jefferson* (Princeton: Princeton University Press, 1950-) 14:420 (hereafter *Papers*).

3   TJ to Peter Carr, September 7, 1814, in Andrew A. Lipscomb and Albert Ellery Bergh, eds., *The Writings of Thomas Jefferson* (Washington, D.C.: Thomas Jefferson Memorial Foundation, 1905) 19:213 (hereafter L&B).

4   Sir William Berkeley, "Report to the Commissioners of Trade and Plantations, 1671," in William Walter Hening, ed., *The Statutes at Large; Being a Collection of All the Laws of Virginia, from the First Session of the Legislature, in the Year 1619* (Richmond, VA: Samuel Pleasants, Jr., 1810-1823), 2:511-517.

5   Ibid. In spite of declaring that Virginia did not have any free schools, Governor Berkeley certainly was aware of the existence of such "free schools" as had been established by the benevolence of Benjamin Symes in 1634 and Dr. Thomas Eaton, brother of Harvard's first president, Nathaniel Eaton, in 1659. Berkeley had signed the bills giving birth to these academies. On early education in Virginia, see Cornelius J. Heatwole, *A History of Education in Virginia* (New York: The Macmillan Co., 1916); William A. Maddox, *The Free School Idea in Virginia before the Civil War* (New York: Teachers College, Columbia University, 1918); J. L. Blair Buck, *The Development of Public Schools in Virginia, 1607-1952* (Richmond, VA: State Board of Education, 1952).

6   On details of Jefferson's childhood and early schooling, see Dumas Malone, *Jefferson and His Time* (Boston: Little, Brown, & Co., 1948), 1:21-22 and 38-48 (hereafter Malone and volume). On tutorial education, see Philip Vickers Fithian, *Journal & Letters of Philip Vickers Fithian, 1773-1774* (Williamsburg, VA: Colonial Williamsburg, 1943).

7   TJ, Autobiography, January 6, 1821, L&B, 1:1-3; Malone 1:40-48.

8   Ibid.; TJ to Joseph Priestley, January 27, 1800, *Works,* 9:102-05.

9   TJ to John Harvie, January 14, 1760, *Papers,* 1:3; TJ, Autobiography, L&B, 1:3; Malone 1:9-109; Mark R. Wenger, "Thomas Jefferson, the College of William and Mary, and the University of Virginia," *The Virginia Magazine of History and Biography* 3 (July 1995) 339-374 (hereafter VMHB).

10   TJ, Autobiography, L&B, 1:3; Malone 1:53-55.

11   Ibid.; TJ to L. H. Girardin, January 15, 1815, L&B, 14:231-32.

12   John Page to TJ, July 1850, as quoted in Malone 1:58; TJ to Martha Jefferson, May 5, 1787, *Papers*, 11:349; Cf. Jennings L. Wagoner, Jr., *Thomas Jefferson and the Education of a New Nation* (Bloomington, IN: Phi Delta Kappa, 1976), 9-12.

13   Malone 1:90-93.

14   TJ to P. S. Du Pont de Nemours, April 24, 1816, in Merrill D. Peterson, *Thomas Jefferson Writings* (New York: The Library of America, 1984), 1387 (hereafter *Writings).*

[15] TJ to Dr. Vince Utley, March 21, 1819, L&B, 15: 187.

[16] TJ to Nathaniel Burwell, Esq., March 14, 1818, L&B, 15:166. Cf. TJ to Robert Skipwith, August 3, 1771, *Papers*, 1:76-77; TJ to John Adams, July 5, 1814, L&B, 14:147-48; or Lester J. Cappon, ed., *The Adams-Jefferson Letters* (Chapel Hill: University of North Carolina Press, 1959), 2:432-33 (hereafter Cappon).

[17] Henry F. May, "The Enlightenment" in Merrill D. Peterson, ed., *Thomas Jefferson: A Reference Biography* (New York: Charles Scribner's Sons, 1986), 51. Portions of this discussion are drawn from Jennings L. Wagoner, Jr., "Jefferson, Justice, and the Enlightened Society" in Deborah A. Verstegen and James Gordon Ward, eds., *Spheres of Justice in Education* (New York: HarperCollins, 1991), 11-33.

[18] TJ to John Cartwright, June 5, 1824, *Writings*, 1491; TJ, The Declaration of Independence as Adopted by Congress, July 4, 1776, *Papers*, 1:429.

[19] TJ, "Draft of Instructions to the Virginia Delegates in the Continental Congress" (MS text of *A Summary View, &c.*), July 1774, *Papers*, 1:135; TJ to James Madison, December 20, 1787, in James Norton Smith, ed., *The Republic of Letters: The Correspondence between Thomas Jefferson and James Madison, 1776-1826* (New York: W.W. Norton & Co., 1995), 1:511-15 (hereafter Smith).

[20] TJ, "Inaugural Address," March 4, 1801 *Writings*, 492-93; TJ to William Roscoe, December 1820, in Adrienne Koch and William Peden, eds., *The Life and Selected Writings of Thomas Jefferson* (New York: The Modern Library, 1972), 702 (hereafter K&P); TJ to James Madison, December 20, 1787, *Papers*, 12:442.

[21] TJ, Declaration of Independence, *Papers*, 1:429.

[22] TJ to Roger C. Weightman, June 24, 1826, *Writings*, 1517; Malone, 1:179; TJ to John Cartwright, June 5, 1824, *Writings*, 1494.

[23] TJ to George Washington, January 4, 1785 [i.e. 1786], *Papers*, 9:151.

[24] TJ to Henry Lee, May 8, 1825, K&P, 719. Cf. Wagoner, *Education of a New Nation*, 21-23.

[25] TJ, Autobiography, L&B, 1:62-64. Cf. Ralph Lerner, *The Thinking Revolutionary: Principle and Practice in the New Republic* (Ithaca and London: Cornell University Press, 1987), 62.

[26] Wagoner, "Jefferson, Justice and the Enlightened Society," 24; Lerner, *The Thinking Revolutionary*, 62. Complete texts of and notes regarding the Revisal of the Laws 1776-1786 are presented in *Papers*, 2:305-657.

[27] TJ, A Bill for Establishing Religious Freedom, *Papers*, 2:546. The quotation is in TJ, *Notes on the State of Virginia*, William Peden, ed. (Chapel Hill: University of North Carolina Press, [1787], 1954), 159 (hereafter *Notes*). For editor's commentary, see note 7 on 291.

[28] TJ to George Wythe, August 13, 1786, *Papers*, 10:244, emphasis added; TJ to John Adams, October 28, 1813, Cappon, 2:390. Cf. Wagoner, *Education of a New Nation*, 25-30.

[29] TJ, Bill for the More General Diffusion of Knowledge, *Papers*, 2:526-527.

[30] Ibid.; TJ, *Notes*, 147-48.

[31] TJ, Bill for the More General Diffusion of Knowledge, *Papers*, 2:526; Merrill Peterson, *Thomas Jefferson and the New Nation: A Biography* (New York: Oxford University Press, 1970), 147-48.

[32] TJ, Bill for the More General Diffusion of Knowledge, *Papers*, 2:528; William Smith, *A General Idea of the College of Mirania* (New York: Johnson Reprint Co., 1969). Cf. Harold Hellenbrand,

The Unfinished Revolution: Education and Politics in the Thought of Thomas Jefferson (Newark: University of Delaware Press, 1990), 79.

33   TJ, Bill for the More General Diffusion of Knowledge, *Papers*, 2:526, 528.

34   Ibid., 2:528-533; TJ, *Notes*, 146-47.

35   Ibid.

36   Ibid., 147.

37   TJ, Bill for Amending the Constitution of the College of William and Mary, and Substituting More Certain Revenues for Its Support, *Papers*, 2:535-543; TJ, Bill for Establishing a Public Library, *Papers*, 2:544-545.

38   TJ, Autobiography, L&B, 1:71; TJ, Bill for Amending the Charter of the College of William and Mary, *Papers*, 2:535-543.

39   See Peterson, *Thomas Jefferson and the New Nation*, 149. Cf. Robert Polk Thompson, "The Reform of the College of William and Mary, 1763-1780," *Proceedings of the American Philosophical Society* (Philadelphia: The American Philosophical Society, 1971), 187-213 (hereafter APS).

40   TJ to George Wythe, August 13, 1786, *Papers*, 10:245

41   James Madison to TJ, February 15, 1787; Madison to TJ, December 4, 1786; and TJ to Madison, December 20, 1787, *Papers*, 11:152, 10:576, and 12:442.

42   TJ, Bill for the More General Diffusion of Knowledge, *Papers*, 2:535; TJ, Autobiography, L&B, 1:71-72. Norfolk County elected its three aldermen in 1798 and in 1799 "schools were opened in several localities of Norfolk County for the free instruction of children for three years" according to William H. Stewart, *History of Norfolk County, Virginia* (Chicago: Biographical Publishing Company, 1902), 178.

43   TJ to John Adams, October 28, 1813, Cappon, 2:388; TJ, *Notes,* 148.

44   TJ to John Adams, September 4, 1823, Cappon, 2:596.

45   TJ to John Banister, Jr., October 15, 1785, L&B, 5:186-88. Although at this point in time Jefferson thought Rome superior to other seats of learning, a few years later he considered Edinburgh the best in the world. See TJ to Mr. M'Alister, December 22, 1791, ibid., 8:274-75. Cf. Jennings L. Wagoner, Jr., "'That Knowledge Most Useful to Us': Thomas Jefferson's Concept of Utility in the Education of Republican Citizens" in James Gilreath, ed., *Thomas Jefferson and the Education of a Citizen* (Washington, D.C.: Library of Congress, 1999), 115-118.

46   Ibid.; TJ to Charles Bellini, September 30, 1785, L&B, 5:151-54; TJ to George Wythe, August 13, 1786, L&B, 5:396; TJ, First Inaugural Address [March 4, 1801], K&P, 323.

47   TJ to Banister, October 15, 1785, L&B, 5:186-88; Wagoner, "That Knowledge Most Useful to Us," 116-17 and n. 5, 334 for variations on this theme.

48   Ralph Izard to TJ, November 10, 1787, *Papers,* 12:338-40; TJ to Izard, July 17, 1788, *Papers*, 13:372-73; TJ to John Adams, July 5, 1814, Cappon, 2:434.

49   Herbert B. Adams, *Thomas Jefferson and the University of Virginia* (Washington, D.C.: Government Printing Office, 1888), 21-30 (hereafter Adams); Philip Alexander Bruce, *History of the University of Virginia, 1819-1919* (New York: The Macmillan Co., 1920) 5 vols., 1:55-60 (hereafter Bruce); Roy J. Honeywell, *The Educational Work of Thomas Jefferson* (Cambridge: Harvard University Press, 1931), 56-58 (hereafter Honeywell).

50 Ibid.; TJ to Quesnay de Beaurepaire, January 6, 1788, *Papers* 12:499-500. Bruce contended that Jefferson's coolness toward Quesnay's project was occasioned by the fact that he was already contemplating plans for a university "in the shadow of Monticello." Both Bruce and Honeywell credit Quesnay's plan with having influenced Jefferson's plans for establishing separate schools at the University of Virginia and giving the institution a bias toward the sciences, but the direct influence is questionable. Jefferson would have been exposed to these ideas by his familiarity with French educational institutions in any case. Cf. Jennings L. Wagoner, Jr. and Christine Coalwell McDonald, "Mr. Jefferson's Academy: An Educational Interpretation," in Robert M. S. McDonald, ed., *Thomas Jefferson's Military Academy: Founding West Point* (Charlottesville: University of Virginia Press, forthcoming 2004), n. 13.

51 Francois D'Ivernois to TJ, September 5, 1794, *Papers*, 28:123-133; TJ to William Cary Nicholas, November 23, 1794, ibid., 208-09; TJ to Francois D'Ivernois, February 6, 1795, ibid., 262-64. Adams, 45, views this overture as "the historical origin of his [Jefferson's] project for a cosmopolitan university, to be equipped with the best scientific talent that Europe could afford."

52 TJ to George Washington, February 23, 1795, *Papers,* 28:275-78, emphasis added; George Washington to TJ, March 15, 1795, ibid., 306-08. Washington's James River Canal Co. stock went to Liberty Hall Academy in Lexington that became Washington College and today is Washington and Lee University. Washington specified that his Potomac Canal shares should create an endowment for a national university in the Federal City, but that did not come to pass. See Neil M. Shawen, "Thomas Jefferson and a 'National' University: The Hidden Agenda for Virginia," *VMHB* 92 (July 1984) 323. Cf. Wagoner and McDonald, 233-34, ff.

53 Gilbert Chinard, "Jefferson and the American Philosophical Society," *Proceedings of the APS*, 87 (July 1943), 267; TJ to Elbridge Gerry, May 13, 1797, *Papers*, 29:362; TJ to Benjamin Rush, January 22, 1797, ibid., 275.

54 Minutes, December 15, 1797, *Early Proceedings of the APS ... from 1744 to 1838* (Philadelphia: APS, 1884), 265; Merle M. Odgers, "Education and the American Philosophical Society." *Proceedings of the APS,* 87 (July 1943), 12-24. The essays by Smith and Knox are most conveniently found in Frederick Rudolph, ed., *Essays on Education in the Early Republic* (Cambridge: Harvard University Press, 1965), 167-223 and 271-372.

55 Benjamin Rush, "Address to the People of the United States," *The American Museum* (January 1787), 9-11; Rush, "Plan for a Federal University," ibid. (December 1788), 444. See also David Madsen, *The National University: Enduring Dream of the USA* (Detroit: Wayne State University Press, 1966), 16-24. Cf. Wagoner and McDonald, 235-37, ff.

56 Richard D. Brown, "The Idea of an Informed Citizenry in the Early Republic," in David T. Konig, ed., *Devising Liberty: Preserving and Creating Freedom in the New American Republic* (Stanford: Stanford University Press, 1995), 141-77; Rudolph, *Essays*, xi; Peter Onuf, *Jefferson's Empire: The Language of American Nationhood* (Charlottesville: University Press of Virginia, 2000), 2, 7, ff.

57 TJ to [unknown correspondent], September 28, 1821, L&B, 15:339.

58 TJ to Joseph Priestley, January 18, 1800, *Writings,* 1069-72, emphasis in original.

59 TJ to Joseph Priestley, January 27, 1800, ibid., 1072-74. The following discussion tracks closely with Wagoner and McDonald, 237ff.

60 Joseph Priestley to TJ, May 8, 1800, LC and Gilbert Chinard, comp., *The Correspondence of Jefferson and Du Pont de Nemours* (New York: Arno Press, [1931], 1979), 15-18; TJ to Joseph Priestley, August 11, 1800, LC.

61 TJ to Du Pont de Nemours, April 12, 1800, in Chinard, *Correspondence*, 11-12.

62   Du Pont de Nemours, *National Education in the United States*, trans., Bessie Gardner Du Pont (Newark: University of Delaware Press, 1923).

63   John Adams, *Diary and Autobiography of John Adams*, L. H. Butterfield, ed. (Cambridge: Harvard University Press, 1961), 3:467, 441-42. See also Don Higginbotham, "Military Education before West Point" and related essays in McDonald, *Thomas Jefferson's Military Academy*.

64   John M. Palmer, *Washington, Lincoln, Wilson: Three War Statesmen* (Garden City, NY: Doubleday, Doran, and Co., 1930), 62-65; TJ, "Memo on Military Academies," April 23, 17[8]3 (misdated 1793), LC. Cf. Wagoner and McDonald, 243-44.

65   TJ, Notes of a Cabinet Meeting on the President's Address to Congress, November 23, 1793, *Papers*, 27: 428.

66   Edgar Denton III, "The Formative Years of the United States Military Academy, 1775-1833" (Ph. D. diss., Syracuse University, 1964) 1-26.

67   Alexander Hamilton to James McHenry, November 23, 1799, in Harold C. Syrett and Jacob E. Cooke, eds., *The Papers of Alexander Hamilton* (New York: Columbia University Press, 1961-87), 24: 69-75.

68   TJ to Joseph Priestley, January 18, 1800, *Writings*, 1070.

69   "An Act Fixing the Military Peace Establishment of the United States," March 16, 1802, *Annals of Congress*, 7th Congress, 1st Session, 1801-1802, 2 *U.S. Statutes*, 1312 (hereafter *Annals);* War Department, List of Officers, July 14, 1801, LC Jefferson's aim to "Republicanize" the army is insightfully developed by Theodore J. Crackel, *Mr. Jefferson's Army: Political and Social Reform of the Military Establishment, 1801-1809* (New York: New York University Press, 1987), chapter 2. See also Crackel, *West Point: A Bicentennial History*, (Lawrence: University Press of Kansas, 2002) 38-51 and Donald Jackson, "Jefferson, Meriwether Lewis, and the Reduction of the United States Army," *Proceedings of the APS*, 124 (April 1980), 91-96.

70   TJ to Peter Carr, September 7, 1814, *Writings*, 1346-52.

71   Dorothy S. Zuersher, "Benjamin Franklin, Jonathan Williams, and the United States Military Academy," (Ph.D. diss., University of North Carolina at Greensboro, 1974), 60-82 (hereafter Zuersher); TJ to Jonathan Williams, July 3, 1796, *Papers*, 29: 139-40; Jonathan Williams to TJ, March 7, 1801 and TJ to Jonathan Williams, March 14, 1801, LC. Williams's other translation was *The Elements of Fortification* published by the War Office in 1800 and, following a fire that destroyed the War Office that year, again in 1801. See Crackel, *West Point*, n. 47, 303.

72   *Annals*, 1312; Denton, 24-28; Zuersher, 89-95.

73   Jonathan Williams to Major Decius Wadsworth, May 13, 1802, Williams to Henry Dearborn, February 14, 1802, Dearborn to Williams, May 31, 1802, Dearborn to Williams, July 9, 1802, and Dearborn to Williams, June 5, 1805, in Jonathan Williams Papers, United States Military Academy Library, (hereafter Williams Papers, USMA Library).

74   Papers of the United States Military Philosophical Society, New York Historical Society (hereafter Papers, USMPS).

75   Constitution of the United States Military Philosophical Society, November 12, 1802 and Jonathan Williams to TJ, December 12, 1802, LC; See also Sidney Forman, "The United States Military Philosophical Society, 1802-1813: Scientia in Bello Pax," *William and Mary Quarterly*, 3rd ser., 2 (July 1945), 273-85 and Forman, *West Point: A History of the United States Military Academy* (New York: Columbia University Press, 1950), 20-35; Peter Michael Molloy, "Technical Education and the Young Republic: West Point as America's *Ecole Polytechnique*, 1802-1833"

(Ph.D. diss., Brown University, 1975) 287-88; Stephen E. Ambrose, *Duty, Honor, Country: A History of West Point* (Baltimore: Johns Hopkins University Press, [1966], 1999), 30-32.

76   Jonathan Williams to TJ, December 12, 1802, LC; TJ to Williams, December 25, 1802, LC.

77   See Jonathan Williams, "Report on Circumstances Regarding his Resigning from the Corps of Engineers," ms., Williams Papers, USMA Library; Zuersher, 105-07; Forman, *West Point*, 26-29.

78   Jonathan Williams to TJ, June 18, 1805, Papers, USMPS; TJ to Williams, July 14, 1805, LC; Williams to TJ, February 6, 1806, TJ to Williams, February 23, 1806, and Joel Barlow to TJ, February 12, 1806, USMPS Papers, USMA Library.

79   See Molloy, 287-88; Forman, *West Point*, 31; Ambrose, 32; Constitution of the USMPS, LC.

80   Jonathan Williams to Henry Dearborn, Report to Congress, March 18, 1808, *Annals*, 2807-12.

81   Ibid.; Molloy, 319-26.

82   TJ, Special Message to Congress, March 18, 1808, L&B, 3:471-72; TJ to Jonathan Williams, October 28, 1808, Williams to TJ, October 31, 1808, and TJ to Williams, November 23, 1808, LC.

83   Joel Barlow to TJ, September 15, 1800, LC; "Further Extracts from Mr. Barlow's Pamphlet," *The National Intelligencer*, November 26, 1806.

84   Joel Barlow to TJ, February 23, 1806, LC; TJ to Barlow, February 24, 1806, *Writings*, 1160. Barlow's *Prospectus*, initially published in *The National Intelligencer*, August 1, November 24, and November 26, 1806, can be found in William K. Bottorff and Arthur Ford, eds., *The Works of Joel Barlow*, 2 vols. (Gainesville, FL: Scholars' Facsimiles and Reprints, 1970).

85   TJ, Sixth Annual Message, December 2, 1806, *Writings*, 529-31; Honeywell, 62-64.

86   TJ to Joel Barlow, December 10, 1807, LC. See also James Woodress, *A Yankee's Odyssey: The Life of Joel Barlow* (Philadelphia: Lippincott, 1958), 241-43.

87   TJ to Jared Mansfield, February 13, 1821, LC.

88   Robert Brent to TJ, August 6, 1805, and TJ to Brent, August 14, 1805, LC. Samuel Yorke At Lee, *History of the Public Schools of Washington City, D.C.* (Washington, D.C.: Board of Trustees of Public Schools, 1876), 1-9.

89   TJ to Joseph C. Cabell, January 31, 1814, *Letters*, 21.

90   TJ to P. S. Du Pont de Nemours, March 2, 1809, *Writings*, 1203; TJ to George Gilmer, August 12, 1787, *Papers*, 12:26.

91   Peterson, *Thomas Jefferson and the New Nation*, 922-924; Jack McLaughlin, *Jefferson and Monticello: The Biography of a Builder* (New York: Henry Holt and Co., 1988), 377. Jefferson's daughter, Martha, her husband, Thomas Mann Randolph, and their eleven children lived at Monticello. Another grandson, Francis Eppes, son of daughter Maria and John Wayles Eppes, was also sometimes in residence.

92   TJ to John Tyler, May 26, 1810, *Writings*, 1226-27.

93   TJ to Mr. [Marc Auguste] Pictet, February 5, 1803, L&B, 10:355.

94   St. George Tucker, "Sketch of a Plan for the Endowment and Establishment of a State-University, in Virginia," Tucker-Coleman Papers, Swem Library, College of William and Mary.

95   Neil McDowell Shawen, "The Casting of a Lengthened Shadow: Thomas Jefferson's Role in Determining the Site for a State University in Virginia," (Ed.D. diss., George Washington University, 1980), 99-100 (hereafter Shawen); Richard Beale Davis, *Intellectual Life in Jefferson's Virginia, 1790-1830* (Chapel Hill: University of North Carolina Press, 1964), 61-62; Littleton W. Tazewell to TJ, December 24, 1804, LC. On TJ comparing reform to giving medicine, see the epigram for Chapter 9.

96   TJ to Littleton Waller Tazewell, January 5, 1805, *Writings,* 1149-50.

97   Ibid., 1150-52.

98   William Arthur Maddox, *The Free School Idea in Virginia Before the Civil War,* (New York: Arno Press, 1969), 47-9 (hereafter Maddox); Bruce, 1:86; Douglas R. Egerton, *Charles Fenton Mercer and the Trial of National Conservatism,* (Jackson and London: University Press of Mississippi, 1989), 117; Honeywell, 15; Shawen, 119.

99   Joseph C. Cabell to Isaac A. Coles, February 22, 1807, Cabell Family Papers, University of Virginia. For additional detail on Cabell's conversion to Jefferson's cause, see Shawen, 107-116.

100 *House Journals,* December 14, 1812, as quoted in Maddox, 49-50, emphasis in original.

101 TJ to Dr. Thomas Cooper, January 16, 1814, L&B 14:59-60; TJ to Joseph Cabell, January 17, 1814 and January 31, 1814, ibid., 70 and 84; TJ to Cooper, August 25, 1814, ibid., emphasis in original, 173-75. See also TJ to Cooper, October 7, 1814, ibid., 199-202. For Cooper's reply to TJ's request for curriculum suggestions, see Cooper to TJ, September 22, 1814, LC.

102 TJ to John Adams, July 5, 1814, Cappon, 2:434, emphasis in original.

103 Bruce, 1:121; Honeywell, 15. Minutes of the Albemarle Academy Board of Trustees, March 25, April 5, 1814, in *Letters,* 379-380 At a subsequent meeting on May 3 (that TJ did not attend), he, his son-in-law Thomas M. Randolph, and Peter Carr were appointed a committee to draft petitions to the legislature asking for an appropriation of money arising from the sale of glebe lands, *Letters,* 381.

104 "Invited himself" is the insightful wording used by Cameron Addis, *Jefferson's Vision for Education, 1760-1845* (New York: Peter Lang, 2003), 30.

105 TJ to Littleton Tazewell, January 5, 1805, *Writings,* 1149-50; TJ to Messrs. Hugh L. White and Others, May 6, 1810, ibid., 1222-23; Minutes of the Albemarle Academy Board of Trustees, August 19, 1814, *Letters,* 382-83. Jefferson's drawings can be found in Patricia C. Sherwood and Joseph Michael Lasala, "Education and Architecture: The Evolution of the University of Virginia's Academical Village," in Richard Guy Wilson, ed., *Thomas Jefferson's Academical Village: The Creation of an Architectural Masterpiece* (Charlottesville: University Press of Virginia, 1993), 12-13 (hereafter Sherwood and Lasala); Frank Edgar Grizzard, Jr., 'Documentary History of the Construction of the Buildings of the University of Virginia, 1817-1818," (Ph.D. diss., University of Virginia, 1996).

106 TJ to John Adams, July 5, 1814, Cappon, 2:434; TJ to Thomas Cooper, August 25, 1814, L&B, 14:173-74, emphasis in original.

107 TJ to Peter Carr, September 7, 1814, *Writings,* 1346-1352.

108 Ibid.

[109] Ibid. Cf. John Locke, *Some Thoughts Concerning Education*, John W. and Jean S. Yolton, eds. (New York: Oxford University Press [1693], 1969).

[110] TJ to Peter Carr, September 7, 1814, *Writings*, 1346-1352. On the necessity of making military instruction a regular part of college education, see TJ to James Monroe, June 18, 1813, L&B, 13:261 as well as his later curricular prescriptions for the University of Virginia. "Ideology," the study of doctrines underlying political and economic systems, was a concept Jefferson borrowed from the political theorist Antoine Destutt de Tracy, whose treatise *Elements of Ideology* was published in France in 1801.

[111] TJ to Thomas Cooper, October 7, 1814, L&B 14:200; Adams, 61.

[112] See n. 103, above; Bruce, 1:128; Shawen, 130, 139.

[113] George W. Randolph to Professor [James L.] Cabell, February 27, 1856, Cabell Papers, University of Virginia; Sherwood and Lasala, 14; Shawen, 140-41. Students from Jefferson College in Pennsylvania sent TJ a congratulatory letter upon his retirement from the presidency in 1809, but the prior claim of this college on Jefferson's name did not figure into his reasons for not wanting to apply that name to his Virginia institution. See Students of Jefferson College to TJ, March 4, 1809, LC.

[114] TJ to John Wood, August 5, 1815, LC; TJ to Joseph Cabell, January 5, 1815, *Letters*, 35-38; Adams, 65; TJ to Correia da Serra, December 27, 1814, L&B, 14: 223-24.

[115] Joseph Cabell to TJ, March 5, 1814, *Letters*, 40; Joseph Cabell to Isaac A. Coles, December 18, 1816, Cabell Papers, University of Virginia; Shawen, 144-45.

[116] Joseph Cabell to TJ, January 16, 1816, *Letters*, 43.

[117] Ibid., 43-44; TJ to Joseph Cabell, January 24, 1816, *Letters*, 47-49; Joseph Cabell to TJ, February 21, 1816, *Letters*, 57-58.

[118] TJ to Joseph Cabell, January 24, 1816, *Letters*, 49.

[119] Ibid.; Shawen, 148-51; "An Act for Establishing a College in the County of Albemarle," [February 14, 1816], in *Letters*, 391-93.

[120] Frank Carr to the Governor [Wilson C. Nicholas], March 25, 1816, in *Calendar of the Virginia State Papers and Other Manuscripts*, 11 vols. (Richmond: Superintendent of Public Printing, 1875-1893), 10:437; Malone, 6:250; Shawen, 183-84; Bruce, 1:142-44.

[121] TJ to George Ticknor, November 25, 1817, LC.

[122] Joseph Cabell to TJ, January 12, 1817, *Letters*, 72-73, emphasis in original.

[123] Bruce, 1:168.

[124] Ibid., 169; Sherwood and Lasala, 15; Malone, 6:255, n. 10 notes that "Kelly's land included a ridge on the approximate line of Preston Ave., which is to the northeast of the University grounds."

[125] Bruce, 1:168-172; Malone, 6:256; "Minutes of the Visitors of Central College," May 5, 1817, in *Letters*, 394. Garrett was appointed soon afterward to fill the position of treasurer as well as proctor.

[126] "Subscriptions to the Central College from persons residing in the country of Albemarle and in other counties and places," *Letters*, 404-12; Joseph Cabell to TJ, August 18, 1817, *Letters*, 78; Bruce, 1:172-78. The name of John Neilson, another master carpenter who worked on Monticello and the University, does not appear on the subscription list.

127 TJ to William Thornton, May 9, 1817, photoengraving, L&B, 17: after 396; TJ to Benjamin Latrobe, June 12, 1817, LC.

128 Bruce, 1:184-86; Sherwood and Lasala, 16-21; William Thornton to TJ, May 27, 1817, LC; Malone, 6:265.

129 Bruce, 1:259-61; Benjamin Latrobe to TJ, June 9 and 12, 1817, as cited by Sherwood and Lasala, 17; Latrobe to TJ, June 17, 1817, LC; Latrobe to TJ, June 28, 1817, LC.

130 TJ to John Hartwell Cocke, July 19, 1817, LC; "Minutes of the Visitors," July 28, 1817, Letters, 396.

131 Bruce, 1:189-90; Richmond Enquirer, October 10, 1817.

132 Malone, 6:264; "Minutes of the Visitors," July 28, 1817, Letters, 396.

133 "Minutes of the Visitors," October 7, 1817, Letters, 396-397; TJ to Thomas Cooper, September 1, 1817, Jefferson Papers, Alderman Library, University of Virginia (hereafter U.Va.); Bruce, 1:193-198.

134 Joseph Cabell to TJ, February 22, 1819, Letters, 165-66; Bruce, 1:193-197; Addis, Jefferson's Vision for Education, 84.

135 Maddox, 63; Bruce, 1:86; Malone, 6:249; Richmond Enquirer, March 2, 1816.

136 Joseph Cabell to TJ, January 24, 1816, Letters, 50-51; Cabell to TJ, February 21, 1816, Letters, 60.; Cabell to TJ, February 26, 1816, Letters, 61.

137 Joseph Cabell to TJ, February 26, 1816, Letters, 61; Virginia Laws, 1815-1816, February 24, 1816, as quoted in Shawen, 155; "An Act for establishing a College in the county of Albemarle," in Acts of the General Assembly, 1815-16, February 14, 1816, 191.

138 Joseph Cabell to TJ, February 26, 1816, Letters, 61.

139 TJ to Wilson Cary Nicholas, April 2, 1816, LC (extract in Honeywell, 230-32); Adams, 73-74.

140 "Report and Digest of the President and Directors of the Literary Fund," Sundry Documents on the Subject of a System of Public Education for the State of Virginia (Richmond: Ritchie, Trueheart, and Du-Val, 1817); Adams, 74-79, emphasis in original; Shawen, 160-61.

141 Ibid.; Adams, 78.

142 "Report and Digest;" Honeywell, 18; TJ to Joseph Cabell, February 2, 1816, Letters, 54.

143 See Maddox, 63-75; Shawen, 160-180; Richmond Enquirer, February 15, 1817.

144 Adams, 79-81; TJ to Joseph Cabell, October 24, 1817, Letters, 84; Malone, 6:268; Shawen, 174.

145 TJ to Joseph Cabell, September 9, 1817, Letters, 79; TJ to J. Correia da Serra, November 25, 1817, L&B, 15:156; [TJ], A Bill for Establishing a System of Public Education, 1817, Honeywell, 233-43 and Letters, 413-427. Shawen, 218-30, provides a detailed comparison of the 1779 and 1817 bills, as does Honeywell, 276-55.

146 TJ to Cabell, September 10, 1817, Letters, 80; TJ to the Honorable, the Speaker of the House of Delegates, January 6, 1818, Letters, 400-04; Shawen, 205-212; Richmond Enquirer, February 10, 1818.

147   Joseph Cabell to TJ, January 23, 1818, *Letters*, 111; ibid., February 1, 1818, *Letters*, 112; ibid., February 13, 1818, *Letters*, 122; ibid., February 20, 1818, *Letters*, 125; Maddox, 74. The law is reprinted in Honeywell, 427-432.

148   TJ to Joseph Cabell, February 7, 1826, *Letters*, 366.

149   TJ to Albert Gallatin, February 15, 1818, L&B, 19:258; Joseph Cabell to James Madison, February 16, 1818, James Madison Papers, LC; cf. Shawen, 248-49.

150   Joseph Cabell to TJ, February 22, 1818, and TJ to Cabell, February 26, 1818, *Letters*, 127 and 128.

151   Joseph Cabell to TJ, February 20, 1818, February 22, 1818, March 11, 1818, and March 15, 1818, *Letters*, 126, 127, 129, and 130-31; Richmond *Enquirer*, March 20, 1818; Bruce, 1:209-11; Shawen, 260-62; A list of all commissioners can be found in Paul Brandon Barringer, *University of Virginia: Its History, Influence, Equipment and Characteristics*, 2 vols. (New York: Lewis Publishing Co., 1904), 1:56 (hereafter Barringer).

152   "An Act Appropriating Part of the Revenue of the Literary Fund, and for Other Purposes," February 21, 1818, *Letters*, 430; Malone, 6:276-77.

153   Adams, 86-87; Malone, 6:278; TJ to James Madison, April 11, 1818 and June 28, 1818, LC.

154   Joseph Cabell to TJ, March 15, 1818, *Letters*, 130; Bruce, 1:216-17; Adams, 87-88.

155   Joseph Cabell to TJ, July 30, 1818, *Letters*, 132-33; Bruce, 1:217.

156   John G. Jackson to Joseph Cabell, December 13, 1818 and George Wythe Randolph to James L. Cabell, February 27, 1856, Cabell Papers, U.Va.; Malone, 6:276-77; Bruce, 1:215, 220. Neither Jefferson's map nor his list of octogenarians has been located by scholars. However, the record amply verifies the existence of the map and Jefferson's calculations. See, for example, Joseph Cabell to TJ, December 24, 1818 and TJ to Cabell, January 1, 1819, *Letters*, 144 and 146.

157   "Proceedings of the Board," Barringer, 1:56; Richmond *Enquirer*, August 11, 1818. The "Report of the Commissioners Appointed to Fix the Site of the University of Virginia, &c." (hereafter Rockfish Gap Report) is most conveniently found in *Letters*, 432-447 or Honeywell, 248-260.

158   TJ to Martha Jefferson Randolph, August 21, 1818, *The Family Letters of Thomas Jefferson*, Edwin M. Betts and James A. Bear, Jr. eds. (Charlottesville: University Press of Virginia, 1966), 426; Malone, 6:279, suggests that Jefferson probably contacted a staphylococcus infection at the baths.

159   Joseph Cabell to TJ, October 24, November 18, November 20, December 8, December 14, December 17, 1818, *Letters*, 133, 134, 136, 137, 138-39, 139-40, 141

160   Joseph Cabell to TJ, December 24, 1818, *Letters*, 141-44.

161   TJ to Joseph Cabell, January 1, 1819, *Letters*, 145-46.

162   Joseph Cabell to TJ, January 18, 1819, *Letters*, 152.

163   Joseph Cabell to TJ, January 7, January 18, January 21, January 25, and February 15, 1819, *Letters*, 147-49, 149-52, 152; 153, and 161; TJ to Cabell, February 19, 1819, *Letters*, 164; Malone, 6:282, 365-66.

164   TJ to Joseph Cabell, January 28; Cabell to TJ, [February] 4 (misdated December), 1818, *Letters*, 154 and 155

165 TJ to Antoine Destutt de Tracy, December 26, 1820, LC.

166 TJ to Joseph Cabell, January 22, 1820, LC. An incomplete version of this letter is in *Letters,* 178.

167 TJ to Joseph Cabell, November 28, 1820, and December 22, 1824; *Letters,* 185-86 and 321-22.

168 TJ to Joseph Cabell, January 31, 1821, *Letters,* 201-02. On Jefferson's architectural designs and construction of the University, see Wilson and Grizzard cited in endnote 105.

169 TJ to Joseph Cabell, January 31, 1821, and December 28, 1822, *Letters,* 201-02 and 260-61.

170 Ibid.; TJ to Antoine Destutt de Tracy, December 26, 1820, LC; TJ to William Roscoe, December 27, 1820, LC; Malone 6:375; TJ to John Holmes, April 22, 1820, *Works,* 10:157.

171 Joseph Cabell to TJ, February 25, 1821, March 10, 1821, and February 3, 1823, *Letters,* 208, 209, and 273. For an extensive study of the opposition to Jefferson's plans, see Robert Orvis Woodburn, "An Historical Investigation of the Opposition to Jefferson's Educational Proposals in the Commonwealth of Virginia." (Ph. D. diss., American University, 1974).

172 Bruce, 1:287, 297.

173 TJ to William Roscoe, December 27, 1820, LC.

174 Rockfish Gap Report, Honeywell, 249-50.

175 A Bill for Establishing a System of Public Education, 1817, Honeywell, 234-35; Wagoner, "Jefferson, Justice and the Enlightened Society," 27-28.

176 TJ to Edward Carrington, January 16, 1787, *Writings,* 880.

177 Onuf, *Jefferson's Empire,* 119; TJ to James Madison, December 20, 1787, *Papers,* 12:442; TJ to Uriah Forrest, with Enclosure, December 31, 1787, *Papers,* 12:478.

178 Rockfish Gap Report, Honeywell, 250.

179 TJ to John Adams, October 28, 1813, Cappon, 2:388; TJ to Peter Carr, August 10, 1787, *Papers,* 12:15.

180 Regulations Adopted by the Board of Visitors of the University of Virginia, October 4, 1824 (hereafter Regulations); Honeywell, 272; Malone, 6:417. Prizes of medals and books were awarded to graduates who might be termed "honorable mention" but less than "highly meritorious" students.

181 TJ to Joseph Priestley, January 18, 1800, *Writings,* 1071; TJ to Nathaniel Bowditch, October 26, 1818, LC; George Ticknor to TJ, October 14, 1815, LC; TJ to Ticknor, October 25, 1818, LC.

182 Bruce, 1:340; TJ to Richard Rush, April 26, 1824, LC.

183 TJ to George Blaettermann, April 26, 1824, LC: Bruce, 1:341, 359; 2:90.

184 Malone, 6:409-10; 416. Board of Visitors, "Organization and Government of the University," April 7, 1824, Honeywell, 269.

185 TJ to Joseph Cabell, April 21, 1826, *Letters,* 377; Bruce, 2:101-105; Honeywell, 106-33.

186 Joseph Cabell to TJ, January 29, 1824, and TJ to Cabell, February 23, 1824, *Letters,* 288-290 and 291-92; Honeywell, 281, 270.

[187] See, for example, TJ to Nathaniel Bowditch, October 26, 1818, LC; TJ to Joseph Cabell, February 3, 1825, *Letters,* 339.

[188] TJ to Benjamin Rush, September 23, 1800, LC; TJ to James Madison, February 1, 1825, Smith, 3:1995; TJ to Joseph Cabell, February 3, 1825, *Letters,* 339; TJ to Madison, February 8, 1825 and February 12, 1825, Smith, 3:1924-26; University of Virginia Board of Visitors Minutes, March 4, 1825, U.Va.; Malone, 6:417; Peterson, *Thomas Jefferson and the New Nation,* 986.

[189] TJ to Joseph Cabell, February 3, 1825, *Letters,* 339; Peterson, ibid., 986-87; Malone, 6:418. A more critical appraisal is offered by Leonard W. Levy, *Jefferson and Civil Liberties* (Cambridge: Harvard University Press, 1963).

[190] TJ to George Ticknor, July 16, 1823, L&B, 15:455; Regulations, October 4, 1824, Honeywell, 272.

[191] Charles W. Eliot, "Address at Southwestern Association of Northern Colleges, San Antonio," San Antonio *Express* , February 27, 1909, clipping, Eliot Papers, Harvard University, Box 273. TJ credited William and Mary with employing a system of free election in a letter to his grandson, Francis Wayles Eppes, November 17, 1821, Betts and Bear, eds., *Family Letters,* 441.

[192] Board of Visitors, To the President and Directors of the Literary Fund, October 7, 1822, *Letters,* 474.

[193] Ibid., 474-75; Honeywell, 168.

[194] TJ to Benjamin Rush, April 21, 1803, L&B, 10:380; TJ to William Short, April 13, 1820 and October 19, 1822, LC; John Hartwell Cocke to Joseph Cabell, March 1, 1819, and Joseph Cabell to Cocke, March 6, 1819, Cabell Papers, U.Va.; Addis, *Jefferson's Vision for Education,* 68-87; Bruce, 2:366-69, 370-71; Malone, 6:376-77.

[195] TJ to Thomas Cooper, November 2, 1822, LC.

[196] Rockfish Gap Report, Honeywell, 257; Robley Dunglison, "The Autobiographical Ana of Robley Dunglison, M.D.," *Transactions of the American Philosophical Society,* Samuel X. Radbill, M.D., ed., (1963) 53:29-30. On Jefferson's views of paternal affection in education, see Hellenbrand, *The Unfinished Revolution.*

[197] Jennings L. Wagoner, Jr., "Honor and Dishonor at Mr. Jefferson's University: The Antebellum Years," *History of Education Quarterly,* 26 (Summer, 1986), 155-180.

[198] TJ to Martha Jefferson, May 21, 1787, Betts and Bear, eds., *Family Letters,* 41; Wagoner, "'That Knowledge Most Useful to Us,'" 123-25.

[199] TJ to Robert Pleasants, undated fragment [August 27, 1796], LC; Lucia Stanton, *Slavery at Monticello* (Charlottesville, Va.: Thomas Jefferson Foundation, 1993), 40.

[200] TJ, *Notes,* 137-139, 162-63; A Bill Concerning Slaves, *Papers,* 2: 470-473; TJ, Autobiography, L&B, 1:72-73.

[201] John Chesterton Miller, *The Wolf by the Ears* (Charlottesville: University Press of Virginia, 1991), 72. For a good example of Jefferson's written communications with American Indians, see TJ to the Chiefs of the Cherokee Nation, January 10, 1806, L&B, 19:146-149.

[202] Malone, 1:280.

[203] TJ to Samuel Kercheval, July 12, 1816, *Writings,* 1401.

Selected Bibliography

Addis, Cameron, *Jefferson's Vision for Education, 1760-1845*. New York: Peter Lang, 2003.

Brown, Richard D., *Strength of a People: The Idea of an Informed Citizenry in America, 1650-1870*. Chapel Hill: University of North Carolina, 1996.

Bruce, Philip Alexander, *History of the University of Virginia 1819–1919*, 5 vols. New York: The Macmillan Co., 1922.

Conant, James, *Thomas Jefferson and the Development of American Public Education*. Berkeley: University of California Press, 1962.

Dewey, John, *The Living Thoughts of Thomas Jefferson*. Toronto: Cassel, 1946.

Fliegelman, Jay, *Prodigals and Pilgrims: The American Revolution Against Patriarchy*. Cambridge: Cambridge University Press, 1984.

Gilreath, James, *Thomas Jefferson and the Education of a Citizen*. Washington, D.C.: Library of Congress, 1999.

Grizzard, Frank Edgar, "Documentary History of the Construction of the Buildings at the University of Virginia, 1817-1828." Ph.D. diss., University of Virginia, 1996. http://etext.lib.virginia.edu/jefferson/grizzard

Healey, Robert M., *Jefferson on Religion in Public Education*. New Haven: Yale University Press, 1962.

Hellenbrand, Harold, *The Unfinished Revolution: Education and Politics in the Thought of Thomas Jefferson*. Newark: University of Delaware Press, 1990.

Helsep, Robert D., *Thomas Jefferson and Education*. New York: Random House, 1969.

Honeywell, Roy J., *The Educational Work of Thomas Jefferson*. Cambridge: Harvard University Press, 1931.

Lee, Gordon C., ed., *Crusade Against Ignorance: Thomas Jefferson on Education*. New York: Teachers College Press, 1961.

Lewis, Jan, *The Pursuit of Happiness: Family and Values in Jefferson's Virginia*. Cambridge: Cambridge University Press, 1982.

Malone, Dumas, *Jefferson the Virginian*. Vol. 1 of *Jefferson and His Time*. Boston: Little, Brown and Co., 1948.

_____, *The Sage of Monticello*. Vol. 6 of *Jefferson and His Time*. Boston: Little, Brown and Co., 1981.

McDonald, Robert M. S., ed., *Thomas Jefferson's Military Academy: Founding West Point.* Charlottesville: University of Virginia Press, 2004.

Onuf, Peter, ed. *Jeffersonian Legacies.* Charlottesville: University Press of Virginia, 1993.

————, "State Politics and Republican Virtue: Religion, Education, and Morality in Early American Federalism," in Paul Finkelman and Stephen E. Gottleib, eds., *Toward a Useable Past: An Examination of the Origins and Duplications of State Protections of Liberty.* Athens: University of Georgia Press, 1991, 91-116.

Peterson, Merrill D., *Thomas Jefferson and the New Nation: A Biography.* New York: Oxford University Press, 1970.

————, *Thomas Jefferson: A Reference Biography.* New York: Charles Scribner's Sons, 1986.

Shawen, Neil McDowell, "The Casting of a Lengthened Shadow: Thomas Jefferson's Role in Determining the Site for a State University in Virginia." Ed.D. diss., George Washington University, 1980.

————, "Thomas Jefferson and a 'National' University: The Hidden Agenda for Virginia." *Virginia Magazine of History and Biography* 92 (July 1984) 309-335.

Wagoner, Jennings L., Jr., "Honor and Dishonor at Mr. Jefferson's University: The Antebellum Years." *History of Education Quarterly 26 (Summer 1986), 155-180.*

————, and Christine Coalwell McDonald, "Mr. Jefferson's Academy: An Educational Interpretation," in Robert M. S. McDonald, *Thomas Jefferson's Military Academy: Founding West Point.* Charlottesville: University of Virginia Press, 2004.

————, "Jefferson, Justice, and the Enlightened Society," in Deborah A. Verstegen and James Gordon Ward, eds., *Spheres of Justice in Education.* New York: HarperCollins, 1991, 11-33.

————, "'That Knowledge Most Useful to Us': Thomas Jefferson's Concept of Utility in the Education of Republican Citizens," in James Gilreath, ed., *Thomas Jefferson and the Education of a Citizen.* Washington, D.C.: Library of Congress, 1999, 115-133, 333-338.

Wilson, Richard Guy, ed., *Thomas Jefferson's Academical Village: The Creation of An Architectural Masterpiece.* Charlottesville: University Press of Virginia, 1993.

INDEX

Numbers in italics indicate illustrations.

About the Monticello Monograph Series

This series, launched to commemorate the 250th anniversary of Jefferson's birth on April 13, 1993, consists of publications of enduring value on various aspects of Jefferson's diverse interests and legacy.

Also in print and currently available:

THOMAS JEFFERSON: A BRIEF BIOGRAPHY
by Dumas Malone

THE POLITICAL WRITINGS OF THOMAS JEFFERSON
edited by Merrill D. Peterson

SLAVERY AT MONTICELLO
by Lucia Stanton

JEFFERSON'S BOOKS
by Douglas L. Wilson

ARCHAEOLOGY AT MONTICELLO
by William M. Kelso

JEFFERSON AND RELIGION
by Eugene R. Sheridan

FREE SOME DAY: THE AFRICAN-AMERICAN FAMILIES OF MONTICELLO
by Lucia Stanton

JEFFERSON'S WEST: A JOURNEY WITH LEWIS AND CLARK
by James P. Ronda

THE LEVY FAMILY AND MONTICELLO 1834-1923:
SAVING THOMAS JEFFERSON'S HOUSE
by Melvin I. Urofsky

JEFFERSON AND SCIENCE
by Silvio A. Bedini

LETTERS FROM THE HEAD AND HEART: WRITINGS OF THOMAS JEFFERSON
by Andrew Burstein

JEFFERSON AND MONROE: CONSTANT FRIENDSHIP AND RESPECT
by Noble E. Cunningham, Jr.

THE LOUISIANA PURCHASE: JEFFERSON'S NOBLE BARGAIN?
by James E. Lewis, Jr.